Letts
gets you through

ENGLISH LANGUAGE AND LITERATURE

REVISION GUIDE

IAN KIRBY

About this Book

Whether you like to learn by seeing, hearing or doing (or a mix of all three), this unique guide uses three different approaches to help you engage with each topic and revise in a way that suits you. It will reinforce all the skills and concepts on the GCSE 9-1 courses for AQA, Edexcel, OCR and WJEC Eduqas, ensuring you are well prepared for your exams.

Key Features

This guide neatly packages the GCSE course into short revision modules to make planning easy.

- Striking page designs, images and diagrams help you engage with the topics.
- A hands-on revision activity for each module.
- Download the relevant track for an audio walk-through of each module.
- Simple, concise explanations for effective revision.
- Keyword boxes to build vocabulary.
- Quick tests to check your understanding of each module.
- Mind maps summarise the key concepts at the end of each topic and show how they are linked.
- Exam practice questions test how well you have understood the topics. Answers are provided at the back of the book.

Letts GCSE 9-1 English Language and Literature Exam Practice Workbook (ISBN 9780008318321) provides further practice.

Download the FREE audio book from lettsrevision.co.uk/GCSE

Contents

SHAKESPEARE

19TH CENTURY FICTION

MODERN FICTION

Purpose, Audience, Form: PAF

- While you're reading a text, you should try to identify its purpose, audience and form.
- This will help you to understand how and why the author is writing in a certain way.

Purpose

- To understand a text, you need to know what it's doing.
- The three texts below are written to inform, persuade and instruct.
- Other purposes include argue, advise, describe, explain and review.
- You should revise the specific features of writing styles. (A good way to do this is by practising your writing using these styles. See pages 26–37.)

1

DAILY NEWS

World - Business - Finance - Lifestyle - Travel - Sport - Weather

Issue: 240104 THE BEST SELLING NATIONAL NEWSPAPER Est - 1965

First Edition Monday 5th June

Arson at Hospital

Fire workers, yesterday, fought to control a blaze at St Martin's Hospital in Westbury. Police are treating the fire as arson.

2

Hi Mum!

Everything's going well at uni – but I've run out of money! I'm literally living on beans (no toast, it's got that bad). I'm really really sorry but could you just send me £20 to get me to the end of the week?

Cheers Mum, love you lots,

Rach x

3

Perfect Scones

250 g self-raising flour
50 g butter
1tsp baking powder
1 egg
100 ml milk

Cut the butter into small chunks and gently work it into the flour and baking powder until it feels like breadcrumbs.

Mix in the milk and whisked egg to create a dough, then roll out to a thickness of about 3 cm.

Formal ➤
behaving or writing in a serious or respectful manner.
Informal ➤
being more friendly or relaxed.

Audience

- It's important to think who a text is written for, as this will affect how it has been written.
- In the texts opposite, the first one is for anyone interested in the news (but aimed at adults). The second one is specifically to Rachel's mother. The last one is for people who like cooking and want to know how to make scones.
- The audience will affect whether something is **formal** or **informal**.

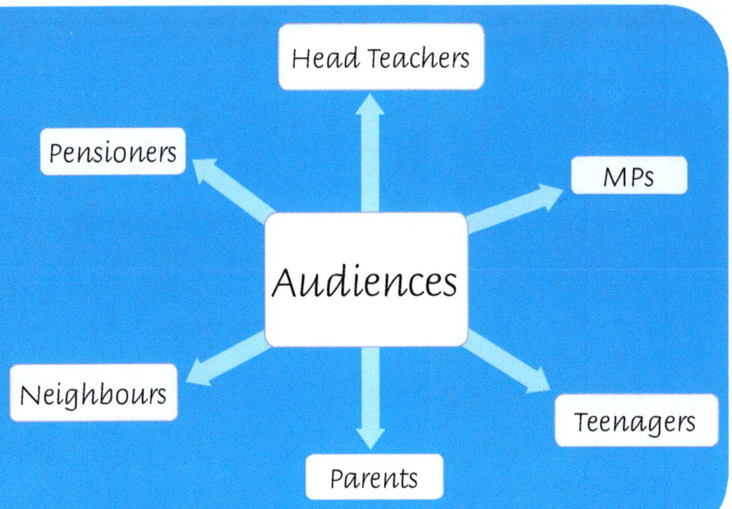

Period

- You should also think about when the text was written.
- Sometimes you will be given modern texts (written in the 20th or 21st century) like the ones opposite.
- Sometimes you will be given older texts, written in the 19th century.
- Older texts will often be more formal, contain longer sentences, and use more unusual and old-fashioned vocabulary.

Form

- You should also think about the form of writing that you've been given: what is it or where would it be found?
- The texts opposite are a newspaper article, an email and a recipe. Each will have been written differently because of what it is.

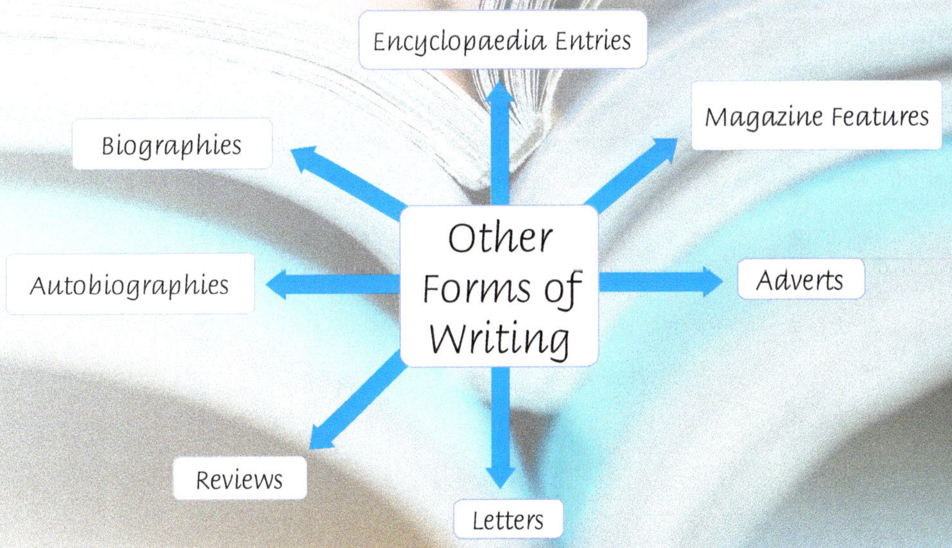

1

Get a magazine (and any junk mail you've been sent) and cut out different examples of texts. Stick them to a sheet of A3 and identify their purpose, form and audience. To develop your skills, underline parts of each text that have helped to reveal the PAF.

1. **What does PAF stand for?**
2. **What different writing purposes are there?**
3. **What different audiences might you encounter?**
4. **What different forms might a text be written in?**

Retrieving Facts

- Facts are things that can be proven by evidence.
- For example: "49 per cent of the people said they like peas." is a fact. However: "Peas taste horrible." is an opinion.
- It's a good idea to look for names or titles (these stand out because they use capital letters), or **statistics** (which stand out because they are numbers). These are all facts.

Retrieving Themed Information

- You will often be given a theme for the information that you need to retrieve.
- This could be anything that is linked to the text you're reading, for example: weather, emotions, old-age.
- You need to think of words that link to the theme you're given and use them to **scan** the text.
- For example, if you're asked to find four things about the weather, you would look out for the word 'weather' and read the sentences in which it appears. But you could also look out for weather-related words such as storm, rain, sun, etc.

Retrieving Opinions

- Opinions are things that people think or feel about something. They are personal rather than based on evidence.
- You can start by looking out for speech marks. These will show you when someone is giving their personal view (such as an interview in a newspaper).
- You should also look out for **adjectives** that offer a judgement, such as words like good, bad, tasty, horrible, etc.

Quoting

- Remember to keep your quotations brief and relevant.
- Selecting a few words that display a feature of language and structure is much better than copying out several lines.

Summarising

- Summarising is all about retrieving the main points in a text.
- You need to write these ideas in your own words to show you actually understand.
- The best way to find main points is to think what the whole text is about, then re-read the beginning of each paragraph. Often, a writer will use a topic sentence to introduce their main idea.
- You will need to use **connectives** to show sequence (e.g. firstly, then, finally), addition (e.g. also, furthermore) and possibly contrast if there are different views to summarise (e.g. however, in comparison).

2

1. Decide what the whole text is about.
2. Re-read the opening sentences of each paragraph.
3. Underline any main points that you find.
4. Quickly number the points you've underlined to give them a logical order.
5. Write out the main points in your own words, joining them with suitable connectives.

Statistics ➤
information based on the collection of data.

Adjectives ➤
describing words.

Scan ➤
find information quickly in a text by searching for key words.

Connectives ➤
words that help to join ideas in different ways.

Find any news article and two highlighter pens. Choose one colour for facts and another for opinions, and highlight the article. To develop your skills, try this again with a different purpose article such as a review. (Do you find more or less opinion? Why might this be?)

1. What is a fact?
2. What is an opinion?
3. Where is the best place to find the main points of a text?
4. Why should you use your own words when summarising?

Features of Language

- Try to use technical terms for features of language. For example: verb (doing word), adverb (word that describes a verb), etc.
- Try to identify any specific techniques. For example: **rhetorical question, second person, repetition,** etc.
- Think about why the writer has used certain words or techniques.

Language and Purpose

- When analysing why the writer has included certain language, you need to consider the purpose of the text. For example:

You're going to love this little gadget – it will change your life!

Purpose	Language	Effect
Persuade	Repeated second person (you)	Grabs the reader's attention
Persuade	Emotive verb (love)	Suggests gadget is great
Persuade	Alliteration (l)	Makes key words stand out

- What you might write:

The writer makes repeated use of the second person as a persuasive technique. Repeating 'you're'/'your' catches the reader's attention, making them feel special and think the product could benefit them.

This is added to by the emotive verb 'love' which persuades the reader that the product is so amazing that they will make an emotional connection with it.

To highlight this, the writer also uses alliteration to persuade, 'love, little, life'. This makes key words stand out: emphasising the emotional connection, how compact it is, and implying a positive effect on the reader's lifestyle.

Sentence Structures for Effect

3

- You should look out for ways in which punctuation can help achieve the writer's purpose. For example:
  - short sentences to emphasise information
  - lists to build up details
  - exclamation marks to highlight a point
  - colons to create a pause and emphasise a fact

Text Structure

- Think about how information is structured to meet its purpose. Consider the start, middle, and end:
  - How does the opening grab the reader and establish the purpose of the text?
  - How does the ending bring the writing to a close and try to achieve some lasting effect on the reader?
  - What features of structure are used to meet the purpose in the rest of the text? For example:

    Do topic sentences establish the main point of each paragraph?

    Are connectives used to show the reader the direction a text is taking?

    Does the message of the text develop or change?

    Does the type of writing change, such as more facts or greater description?

Rhetorical question ➤
a question that is used to make the reader think.

Second person ➤
writing or speaking to your audience directly, using 'you'.

Repetition ➤
using important words more than once to reinforce your meaning.

Make cue cards for different technical terms, such as adjective or second person. Write the term on the front and the definition on the back. Scatter them around the house (although this may annoy the other people you live with!) and, each time you see one, test yourself. To develop this skill, buy some different coloured sticky dots. Allocate a feature of language to a colour and stick them all over a magazine you're reading, each time thinking about the effect of the feature you've identified.

1. **What is a verb, a noun, an adjective, and an adverb?**
2. **What features of sentence structure might you look for in a text?**
3. **What areas should you think about when exploring how a text is structured?**

Reading the Question

- Read the question carefully so you know what you need to specifically compare.
- You will usually be given a theme, such as animals, the environment, etc.
- You might also be given prompts to focus on, such as the writers' language, their use of sentence structure, and how they achieve their purposes.

What to Include

1. Come up with a similarity or difference about how the writers approach the theme.
2. Identify and quote specific features of language or structure used by the writers.
3. Explain how this helps to get across their ideas about the theme.

Connectives

- Use connectives of comparison to show the examiner that you are comparing.

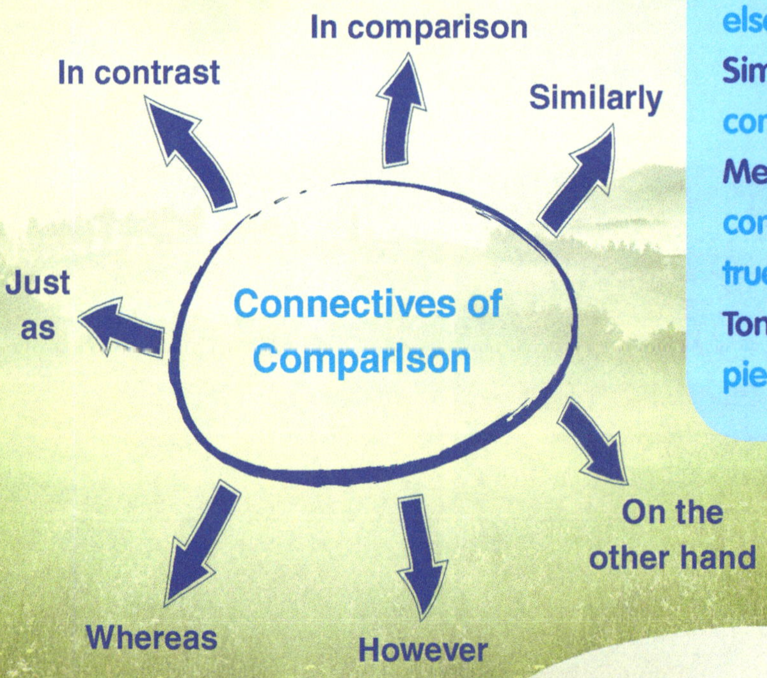

Autobiography ➤ a text written by someone about their own life (whereas a biography is written about someone else's life).

Simile ➤ a descriptive comparison, using like or as.

Metaphor ➤ a descriptive comparison that claims to be true, rather than like or as.

Tone ➤ the emotion in a piece of writing or speech.

4

Coming Up With Ideas

➤ Look at these extracts of modern non-fiction, focussed on mothers. The first is from an **autobiography**, the second is from a speech at an awards ceremony. A student has underlined features of language and structure that stood out to them.

My mother is scraping a piece of burned toast out of the kitchen window, a crease of annoyance across her forehead. This is not an occasional occurrence, a once-in-awhile hiccup in a busy mother's day. My mother burns the toast as surely as the sun rises each morning. In fact, I doubt if she has ever made a round of toast in her life that failed to fill the kitchen with plumes of throat-catching smoke. I am nine now and have never seen butter without black bits in it.

It is impossible not to love someone who makes toast for you. People's failings, even major ones such as when they make you wear short trousers to school, fall into insignificance as your teeth break through the rough, toasted crust and sink into the doughy cushion of white bread underneath.

(from 'Toast' by Nigel Slater)

And last, my mom. I don't think you know what you did. You had my brother when you were 18 years old. Three years later, I came out. The odds were stacked against us. Single parent with two boys by the time you were 21 years old. Everybody told us we weren't supposed to be here. We went from apartment to apartment by ourselves. One of the best memories I had was when we moved into our first apartment, no bed, no furniture and we just sat in the living room and just hugged each other.

You made us believe. You kept us off the street. You put clothes on our backs, food on the table. When you didn't eat, you made sure we ate. You went to sleep hungry. You sacrificed for us.

(speech by Kevin Durant on collecting the NBA's Most Valuable Player Award in 2014)

➤ If you were comparing how these two authors feel about their mothers, you might get some of these ideas. (You could practise writing some up using the simple comparison structure covered on page 10):

- *Both love their mums – emphasised by short sentences.*
- *Slater seems less close to his mum than Durant – mother / mom.*
- *Neither mum had a perfect life. One was annoyed by her inability to cook, the other struggled to support her family – use of* ***metaphor*** *(and* ***simile*** *in the first extract).*
- *Both mums did their best for their boys – shown through list form and powerful verbs.*
- *Both have happy memories of their mothers – description of toast / hugging in apartment.*
- *Slater makes fun of his mum a bit, whilst Durant seems in awe of his mum – use of humour / more serious* ***tone****, repetition, and powerful verbs.*

Find two different texts that have a shared theme. Using a different colour pen for each of your ideas, circle similarities and differences in how the texts approach their theme. To develop this skill, list the different features of language and structure used to get across each writer's idea.

1. **Why do you need to read the question carefully?**
2. **What three things should you include in order to structure your comparisons?**
3. **List three connectives of comparison.**

Things to Remember

- If you have to compare a modern text with a 19th century text, don't panic. It's no different from comparing two modern texts.
- Make sure you read the question carefully, then start looking for points of comparison.
- Don't be put off by the fact that 19th century texts can seem more difficult due to longer sentences, more formal writing and more complex or old-fashioned language.

Exploring Language and Structure

- Look at these extracts of non-fiction. You have already read the first one from Nigel Slater's autobiography 'Toast'. The second is an extract from the diaries of Charles Darwin, who travelled the world and developed the theory of evolution. How do the two writers show their attitudes towards food?

My mother is scraping a piece of burned toast out of the kitchen window, a crease of annoyance across her forehead. This is not an occasional occurrence, a once-in-a while hiccup in a busy mother's day. My mother burns the toast as surely as the sun rises each morning. In fact, I doubt if she has ever made a round of toast in her life that failed to fill the kitchen with plumes of throat-catching smoke. I am nine now and have never seen butter without black bits in it.

It is impossible not to love someone who makes toast for you. People's failings, even major ones such as when they make you wear short trousers to school, fall into insignificance as your teeth break through the rough, toasted crust and sink into the doughy cushion of white bread underneath.

(from 'Toast' by Nigel Slater)

September 16th.

...We did not reach the posta on the Rio Tapalguen till after it was dark. At supper, from something which was said, I was suddenly struck with horror at thinking that I was eating one of the favourite dishes of the country, namely, a half formed calf, long before its proper time of birth. It turned out to be Puma; the meat is very white, and remarkably like veal in taste. Dr. Shaw was laughed at for stating that "the flesh of the lion is in great esteem, having no small affinity with veal, both in colour, taste, and flavour." Such certainly is the case with the Puma. The Gauchos* differ in their opinion whether the Jaguar is good eating, but are unanimous in saying that cat is excellent.

****Gauchos = a group of people native to the South Americas***

(from Charles Darwin's diary, 'The Voyage of the Beagle', 1860)

Possible Ideas

- Both describe liking certain foods: adjectives and metaphor to describe toast; adverb and simile to describe puma.
- Both show dislike towards food: adjectives and **personification** linked to burned toast; adverb and metaphor when Darwin thinks he's eating something horrible.
- Both writers use food to tell the reader about someone: metaphor, simile, short sentence and humour to show his feelings towards his mother; more formal but unusual references to show us how the Gauchos live.

Personification ➤ describing a thing as if it has human qualities.

5

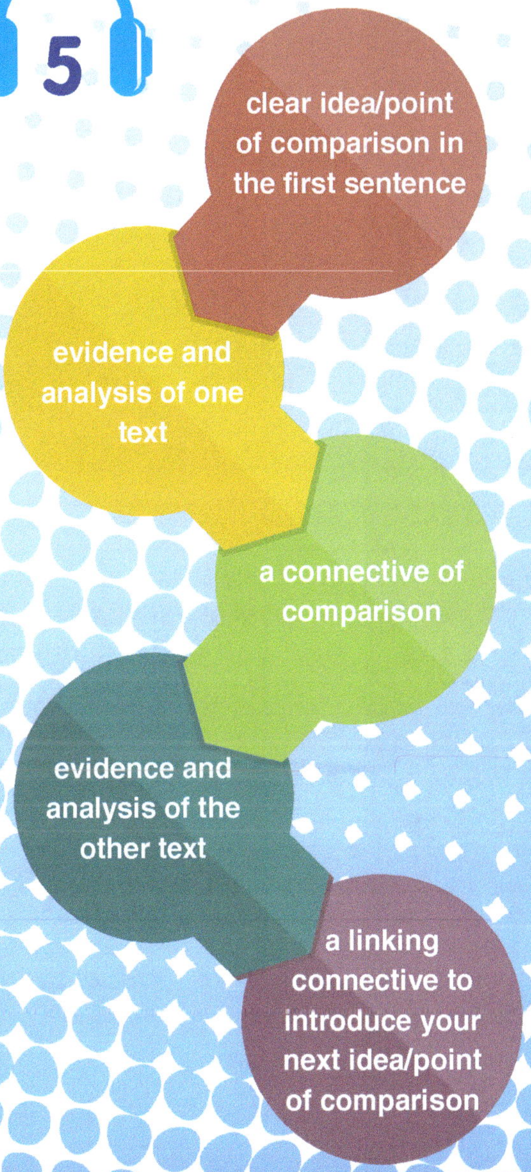

Writing Your Response

- Read the start of a student's response, comparing the attitudes towards food that are shown in the two texts. Notice the way the analysis is structured:

In the two extracts, both Slater and Darwin describe their enjoyment of certain foods. Slater describes eating toast, "rough, toasted crust and sink into the doughy cushion". The adjectives and metaphor describe the contrasting textures of the toast and help us to imagine his pleasure. In comparison, Darwin uses a simple simile to help us imagine the taste of a puma, "remarkably like veal in taste". He adds the adverb to show his surprise at enjoying such an unusual meat.

As well as this, both authors show their dislike of certain foods...

To help you revise the way to compare a text, turn the flow diagram into a mobile that you can hang up. To develop your skills, find two non-fiction texts, annotate them, and then try to analyse them following the structure on your mobile.

1. **What differences might you notice between modern and 19th century writing?**
2. **What do you still need to include when comparing modern and 19th century texts?**
3. **In what ways do you think a diary is similar and different to an autobiography?**

Unseen Non-fiction | Mind Map

Unseen Non-Fiction

- Don't be panicked by 19th century texts: they can just be a bit harder to read. Analyse them in the same way as a modern text.
- Show the examiner you're comparing by using connectives of comparison.
- How is a text structured? Think: start, middle, end.
- Scan a text by looking for key words.
- Don't just identify features of language and structure: analyse how they link to the writer's purpose.
- Remember to establish the purpose, audience and form of any texts you're given.
- Opinions are what people think: look for quotes and value-judgement words.
- State your idea, support it with evidence from the text, explain how your evidence shows your idea.
- Keep your quotations brief.
- Facts can be proven: look for names, titles and statistics.
- When summarising, look for topic sentences at the start of paragraphs.

Read this extract from Morrissey's 'Autobiography' where he describes his school days in 1960s Manchester.

The school looms tall and merciless in central Hulme, as the last of the old order, a giant black shadow of ancient morality since 1842, invoking deliberate apprehension into every wide-eyed small face that cautiously holds back the tears as he or she is left at its steps – into long echoing halls of whitewashed walls, of carbolic and plimsoll and crayon blazing through the senses, demanding that all cheerful thought must now die away. This bleak mausoleum called St Wilfrid's has the power to make you unhappy, and this is the only message it is prepared to give. Padlocks and keys and endless stone stairways, down unlit hallways to darkened cloakrooms where something terrible might befall you.

Children tumble in soaked by rain, and thus they remain for the rest of the day – wet shoes and wet clothes moisten the air, for this is the way. Our teachers, too, are dumped, as we are, in St Wilfrid's parish. There is no money to be had and there are no resources, just as there is no colour and no laughter. These children are slackly shaped and contaminated. Many stragglers stink, and will faint due to lack of food, but there is no such thing as patient wisdom to be found in the sharp agony of the teachers.

Headmaster Mr Coleman rumbles with grumpiness in a rambling stew of hate. He is martyred by his position and is ruled by his apparent loathing of the children. Convincingly old, he is unable to praise, and his military servitude is the murdered child within. His staff stutters on, minus any understanding of the child mind. These educators educate no one, and outside of their occupations they surely lament their own allotted spot? No schoolteacher at St Wilfrid's will smile, and there is no joy to be found between the volcano of resentment offered by Mother Peter, a bearded nun who beats children from dawn to dusk, or Mr Callaghan, the youngest of the crew, eaten up by a resentment that he couldn't control.

1. Select two facts about St Wilfrid's School. (2 marks)
2. In the first paragraph, what feelings does the author describe children having when they first see the school? (2 marks)
3. Select two quotations from the second paragraph that suggest that the children don't have happy lives. Explain your choices. (4 marks)
4. Explain what the headmaster, Mr Coleman, is like. Support your ideas with evidence from the text. (6 marks)
5. Looking at the whole text, how does the author use language and structure to present his feelings about St Wilfrid's School? (12 marks)

Module 1 | Information Retrieval

Read the Question

- This might seem obvious but you need to make sure you know what you're specifically focussing on, so that all the information you retrieve is relevant.
- Examiners can sometimes state where in the text they want you to look: a certain paragraph or specific lines. You won't get marks if you find relevant information but it's from the wrong place.

Synonyms ➤
different words that have the same, or similar, meaning (such as: cold, chilly, freezing).

Facts and Themes

- You could be asked to retrieve facts from a text, such as key information about a character, or you could be asked to retrieve information on a theme, like details about the weather.
- To help you do this, you need to practise scanning a text: looking quickly through a text to spot relevant words, then reading the surrounding sentences in order to clarify the information.
- For facts, look for capital letters (this could indicate names of people or places) and numbers (this could tell you dates or ages).
- For themes, look for the actual word (such as nature) but also **synonyms** and related words (like countryside, wildlife, etc.).

Practise Scanning

➤ Read the text below.

Margaret was struck afresh by her cousin's beauty. They had grown up together from childhood, and all along Edith had been remarked upon by every one, except Margaret, for her prettiness; but Margaret had never thought about it until the last few days, when the prospect of soon losing her companion seemed to give force to every sweet quality and charm which Edith possessed. They had been talking about wedding dresses, and wedding ceremonies; and Captain Lennox, and what he had told Edith about her future life at Corfu, where his regiment was stationed; and the difficulty of keeping a piano in good tune (a difficulty which Edith seemed to consider as one of the most formidable that could befall her in her married life), and what gowns she should want in the visits to Scotland, which would immediately succeed her marriage; but the whispered tone had latterly become more drowsy; and Margaret, after a pause of a few minutes, found, as she fancied, that in spite of the buzz in the next room, Edith had rolled herself up into a soft ball of muslin and ribbon, and silken curls, and gone off into a peaceful little after-dinner nap.

(from 'North and South' by Elizabeth Gaskell)

➤ Scan the text to find four facts about Edith, then find four things that Margaret feels about Edith.

➤ If you looked for capital letters and numbers, you may have found the following facts: Edith's cousin is called Margaret; Edith is going to be marrying Captain Lennox; Edith will be moving to Corfu; Edith will be going to Scotland after her wedding.

➤ If you looked for the word 'Edith' and any adjectives, you may have found the following opinions: Margaret thinks Edith is beautiful; she doesn't want to be parted from her; Edith is sweet and charming; she is innocent (not aware of the difficulties of marriage/how she looks asleep).

6

Working with a friend, challenge each other to find specific information. Get an extract of fiction (the opening of any novel will do), read it yourself, and decide on either a theme of information or a set of facts that your friend has to find. You could use highlighters to help you when scanning. To develop your skills, time each other so you get quicker for the actual exam.

1. **Why do you need to read the question carefully?**
2. **What can help you find facts in a text?**
3. **How can synonyms help you when scanning a text?**

Sentence Structure

- When analysing fiction, you should try to comment on how the writer has used sentence structure to convey meaning. For example:
  - short sentences for shock or emphasis
  - lists to build up ideas
  - dashes or **ellipses** to create dramatic pauses
  - long sentences to convey a lot of detail
  - exclamations or questions to suggest what a character is feeling.

Narrative Structure

- You may also be asked to explore how an extract of fiction is structured. This means what the author has done to establish and develop their writing. Try to think of the extract in terms of its start, middle, and end. For example:
  - How does it begin? Do we get characters, setting, events, or a combination of these?
  - How does this beginning try to engage the reader?
  - What happens in the middle and how does this build on the opening?
  - As the extract progresses, does the reader get answers to certain questions or just more questions?
  - How does the end of the extract engage the reader?

Ellipsis ➤
... used to miss out information.

Suspense ➤
a feeling of exciting uncertainty.

Short sentence to emphasise **suspense**

Long sentence to add detail and establish plot

Dash creates a dramatic pause to emphasise the idea that people have suffered

Last paragraph establishes how the story will be written (different people's experiences)

Long sentences to build up our understanding of the plot

Short sentence to create a dramatic way into the story

In the first part of ROBINSON CRUSOE, at page one hundred and twenty-nine, you will find it thus written:

"Now I saw, though too late, the Folly of beginning a Work before we count the Cost, and before we judge rightly of our own Strength to go through with it."

Only yesterday, I opened my ROBINSON CRUSOE at that place. Only this morning (May twenty-first, Eighteen hundred and fifty), came my lady's nephew, Mr. Franklin Blake, and held a short conversation with me, as follows:—

"Betteredge," says Mr. Franklin, "I have been to the lawyer's about some family matters; and, among other things, we have been talking of the loss of the Indian Diamond, in my aunt's house in Yorkshire, two years since. /.../

"In this matter of the Diamond," he said, "the characters of innocent people have suffered under suspicion already—as you know. The memories of innocent people may suffer, hereafter, for want of a record of the facts to which those who come after us can appeal. There can be no doubt that this strange family story of ours ought to be told. And I think, Betteredge, Mr. Bruff and I together have hit on the right way of telling it."

Very satisfactory to both of them, no doubt. But I failed to see what I myself had to do with it, so far.

"We have certain events to relate," Mr. Franklin proceeded; "and we have certain persons concerned in those events who are capable of relating them. Starting from these plain facts, the idea is that we should all write the story of the Moonstone in turn—as far as our own personal experience extends, and no farther. We must begin by showing how the Diamond first fell into the hands of my uncle Herncastle, when he was serving in India fifty years since. This prefatory narrative I have already got by me in the form of an old family paper, which relates the necessary particulars on the authority of an eye-witness. The next thing to do is to tell how the Diamond found its way into my aunt's house in Yorkshire, two years ago, and how it came to be lost in little more than twelve hours afterwards. Nobody knows as much as you do, Betteredge, about what went on in the house at that time. So you must take the pen in hand, and start the story."

(from 'The Moonstone' by Wilkie Collins)

Suggests something bad may happen

Gradually establishes narrator: well-read, servant, respectful

Establishes date and character / makes it seem more 'real'

Introduces a crime but keeps information brief so the reader wants more

The crime is developed, but still raising questions, through idea of suffering

We're told more about the story of the diamond, getting the reader more intrigued

Betteredge is now going to begin the story; this makes us read on

Pick the opening page of any novel and turn it into a poster flow diagram of how it engages the reader. Use different colours for start, middle, and end. Pick out key quotations and say how they help to establish and develop the opening. To develop your skills, use another colour to comment on the effects of any particular sentence structures in your quotations.

1. What is the difference between sentence structure and narrative structure?
2. What sort of features of sentence structure should you look out for?
3. How can you split an extract into three to help you consider how it develops?

Language

- When the examiner asks you to analyse language, you need to look at the type of words an author uses and how these have an effect on the reader.
- You need to say what the author does, support this with a key quotation, and then analyse how this conveys meaning.

8

Mood

- You could be asked to analyse how mood is created by a writer. This means the atmosphere or emotion in the text, such as sad, scary, or calm.
- In the extract below, the mood could be described as desperately bored. An examiner could ask you how this is achieved by the author.

> The world is full of little towns that people want to leave, and scarcely know why. The hills crowd in too closely, they say, or the plains which stretch around are too featureless, or the freeway runs through, or doesn't run through: you can hardly put your finger on the source of their discontent, or indeed your own. A kind of sorrow creeps along the streets and drags you down; you can hardly lift your feet to shake it off. The shops in the High Street are forever closed for lunch, or would be better if they were: the houses in the centre may be old, veritable antiquities, but still lack resonance: a tuning fork that declines to twang, dead in the face of all expectation. And if nothing happens you know you'll soon be dead as well, or your soul will be.
>
> (from 'Growing Rich' by Fay Weldon)

- You could start by picking out the phrases that link to boredom or desperation. For example: 'A kind of sorrow creeps along the streets and drags you down'.
- Then identify any language features in your phrases. For instance, the quotation above uses **personification** and powerful verbs.
- Then think about how that creates a mood of desperate boredom. For example, the personification makes the whole town seem miserable and dull (added to by the slow verb 'creep'), but also that this mood of boredom is oppressive and gets to everyone (the verb phrase 'drags you down').

What else could you add about how the extract creates a mood of desperate boredom?

Character and Setting

- You could be asked to analyse how an author presents a character and/or setting.
- In the extract below the character could be described as old and creepy.

> We should not have seen so much but for a lighted lantern that an old man in spectacles and a hairy cap was carrying about in the shop. Turning towards the door, he now caught sight of us. He was short, cadaverous, and withered, with his head sunk sideways between his shoulders and the breath issuing in visible smoke from his mouth as if he were on fire within. His throat, chin, and eyebrows were so frosted with white hairs and so gnarled with veins and puckered skin that he looked from his breast upward like some old root in a fall of snow.
>
> (from 'Bleak House' by Charles Dickens)

- If you were focussing on character, you could start by picking out the phrases that describe the character's age or make him sound creepy. For example: 'short, cadaverous, and withered'.
- Identify any language features. For instance, the quotation above uses a pattern of three powerful adjectives.
- Think about how that makes the man seem old or creepy. For example, the pattern of three adjectives highlights the immediate impression the old man has on the narrator. 'Withered' suggests he is very wrinkled and looked as if he is dying. This is emphasised by 'cadaverous', which means he looks like a dead body.

What else could you add about how the extract creates character or setting?

Personification ➤
describing an object or thing as if it has human qualities.

'Explode' a text. Choose the opening page of any novel. Photocopy it, then cut up all the key phrases and stick them to a sheet of A3 under the headings: mood, character, setting.
To develop your skills, use different colours to highlight and analyse the effects of different language features.

1. **What three areas of an unseen fiction text might you be asked to analyse in terms of language?**
2. **How will WHAT and HOW help you to analyse language?**
3. **What sort of features of language might you look out for?**

Getting Ideas for Comparison

- If you're asked to compare two extracts of modern fiction, you'll be given a focus such as how the authors convey character, setting, or mood.
- You'll need to come up with ideas, support them with evidence, and then analyse how the authors' use of language and structure convey meaning.
- To come up with ideas, make a quick mind map or use a Venn diagram. Read the two extracts and look at the Venn diagram created by a student to compare how the authors establish their settings.

It was a bright cold day in April, and the clocks were striking thirteen. Winston Smith, his chin nuzzled into his breast in an effort to escape the vile wind, slipped quickly through the glass doors of Victory Mansions, though not quickly enough to prevent a swirl of gritty dust from entering along with him.

The hallway smelt of boiled cabbage and old rag mats. At one end of it a coloured poster, too large for indoor display, had been tacked to the wall. It depicted simply an enormous face, more than a metre wide: the face of a man of about forty-five, with a heavy black moustache and ruggedly handsome features. Winston made for the stairs. It was no use trying the lift. Even at the best of times it was seldom working, and at present the electric current was cut off during daylight hours. It was part of the economy drive in preparation for Hate Week.

(from 'Nineteen Eighty Four' by George Orwell)

Snowman wakes before dawn. He lies unmoving, listening to the tide coming in, wave after wave sloshing over the various barricades, wish-wash, wish-wash, the rhythm of heartbeat. He would so like to believe he is still asleep.

On the eastern horizon there's a greyish haze, lit now with a rosy, deadly glow. Strange how that colour still seems tender. The offshore towers stand out in dark silhouette against it, rising improbably out of the pink and pale blue of the lagoon. The shrieks of the birds that nest out there and the distant ocean grinding against the ersatz reefs of rusted car parts and jumbled bricks and assorted rubble sound almost like holiday traffic.

Out of habit he looks at his watch – stainless-steel case, burnished aluminium band, still shiny although it no longer works. He wears it now as his only talisman. A blank face is what it shows him: zero hour. It causes a jolt of terror to run through him, this absence of official time. Nobody nowhere knows what time it is.

(ersatz = an inferior substitute)

(from 'Oryx and Crake' by Margaret Atwood)

1984	Both	Oryx and Crake
City – indoor and outside	Neither character seems to like the setting, and there are creepy references to darkness	Coast – outside
Smells used to suggest poverty	Both areas seem rundown/uncared for	Colours used to suggest pollution
Sense of **irony** in the name 'Victory Mansions'	Unusual references to time (suggests the future)	Nature has been ruined

➤ This would give you three points of similarity and three points of contrast. Each point could be written up using a simple structure:

Point about text 1 → **Evidence** → **Analysis** → **Connective of comparison** → **Point about text 2** → **Evidence** → **Analysis**

Irony ➤ saying one thing but actually having the opposite meaning.

9

Working with a friend, give each other a section of any modern novel. Challenge each other to evaluate how good the extract is, but your comments have got to be based on analysis of language and structure. To develop your skills, ask each other to comment on a specific aspect (such as characters you can relate to or a mood that engages you).

1. When comparing, what do you need to use to link your points?
2. What should you do before writing your answer? How?
3. What must you remember to comment on about your chosen quotations?

Unseen Fiction | Mind Map

Unseen Fiction

- Use a simple analysis structure: state a point > support it with evidence > analyse how features of language or structure in your quotation get across the point you made.
- Use mind maps or Venn diagrams to help you form ideas for comparison. Remember connectives to show comparison.
- Features of language = verb, adjective, adverb, pronoun, simile, metaphor, personification, contrast, etc.
- Sentence structure = lists, short sentences, long sentences, exclamations, questions, dashes, etc.
- Scan the text to find information.
  - Use key words and synonyms to find ideas on a theme
  - Use capital letters and numbers to find facts
- Narrative structure = start, middle, and end
  - How does an extract establish characters, settings, and themes?
  - How does an extract develop as it goes on?

Read this opening of the novel 'The Collector' by John Fowles. It is about a man who collects butterflies, but he becomes obsessed with a girl called Miranda.

WHEN she was home from her boarding-school I used to see her almost every day sometimes, because their house was right opposite the Town Hall Annexe. She and her younger sister used to go in and out a lot, often with young men, which of course I didn't like. When I had a free moment from the files and ledgers I stood by the window and used to look down over the road over the frosting and sometimes I'd see her. In the evening I marked it in my observations diary, at first with X, and then when I knew her name with M. I saw her several times outside too. I stood right behind her once in a queue at the public library down Crossfield Street. She didn't look once at me, but I watched the back of her head and her hair in a long pigtail. It was very pale, silky, like burnet cocoons. All in one pigtail coming down almost to her waist, sometimes in front, sometimes at the back. Sometimes she wore it up. Only once, before she came to be my guest here, did I have the privilege to see her with it loose, and it took my breath away it was so beautiful, like a mermaid.

Another time one Saturday off when I went up to the Natural History Museum I came back on the same train. She sat three seats down and sideways to me, and read a book, so I could watch her for thirty-five minutes. Seeing her always made me feel like I was catching a rarity, going up to it very careful, heart-in-mouth as they say. A Pale Clouded Yellow, for instance. I always thought of her like that, I mean words like elusive and sporadic, and very refined – not like the other ones, even the pretty ones. More for the real connoisseur.

Well, then there was the bit in the local paper about the scholarship she'd won and how clever she was, and her name as beautiful as herself, Miranda. So I knew she was up in London studying art. It really made a difference, that newspaper article. It seemed like we became more intimate, although of course we still did not know each other in the ordinary way.

elusive = difficult to find or catch *connoisseur = an expert*

1. Find four facts about Miranda from paragraph 1.
2. How has the writer structured the text in order to engage the reader?
3. How does Fowles use language to show the speaker's obsession with Miranda?
4. How far do you agree that the speaker comes across as frightening rather than romantic?
5. Compare the extract from 'The Collector' with the opening of the modern novel you are studying. How do the two authors present their characters?

Module 1 | Writing to Inform

The Basics

- Always begin by reading the writing task carefully and making sure you understand what you're informing people about, who your specific audience is, and what form you are expected to write in (such as a letter or a magazine article).
- Writing to inform is all about presenting the reader with lots of information in the form of **facts** and **statistics**. This could be a report on a local event, a speech about the work of a charity or a guide to your home town.
- Depending on the task, you'll have to make some of the information up. It's a test of your writing, not how much you know about a local event or a certain charity.

Key Features of Writing to Inform

- You'll usually use the third person and a combination of past and present tense.
- It's very important that you use plenty of **connectives** of time and place, in order to make it clear to your audience where and when things are taking place.
- Focus on facts and evidence rather than feelings and opinions.
- Remember that an audience would be coming to your writing to find out things that they want to know, so you may need to use a combination of positive and negative language in order to tell the whole truth. This is one of the big differences between writing to inform and writing to persuade.

Plan and Structure Your Writing Carefully

- You need to plan your ideas and order them logically so that, when you come to write it, the information is easy to understand. Depending on the task, this might be **chronological** or **thematic**.

Fact ➤ something that can be proven.

Statistic ➤ facts in the form of numbers.

Connective ➤ a joining word.

Chronological ➤ putting events in the order in which they happened.

Thematic ➤ ideas relating to a specific subject.

Example of a Chronological Plan

Task: Write a newspaper article about a car accident on the M1.
→ Summary of what has happened
→ Where, when, what cars crashed
→ How the crash affected other vehicles
→ What the police did
→ Opinions of people caught up in the day's events
→ How long the motorway was closed for and how it affected national traffic

Example of a Thematic Plan

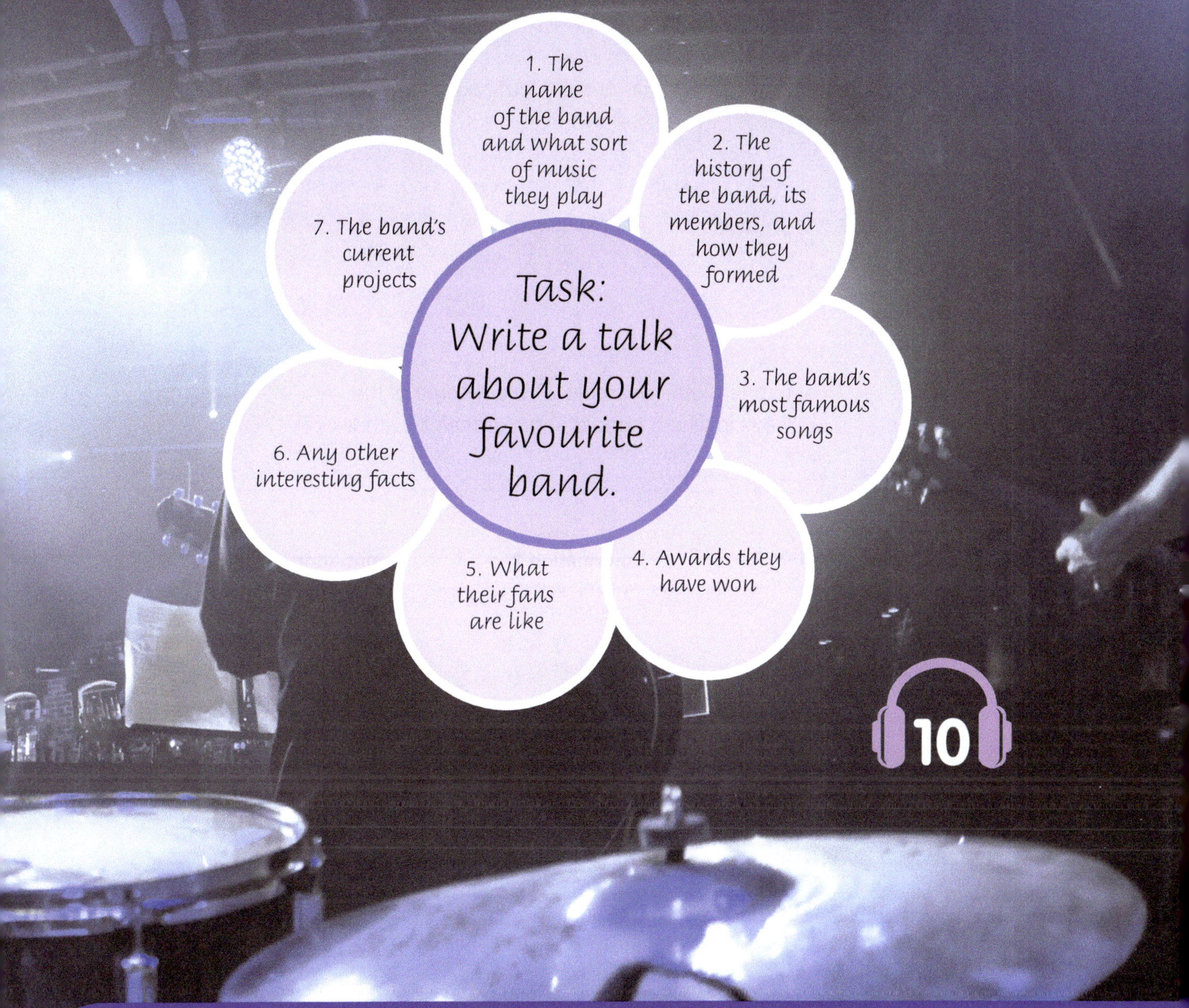

Play reporter for the day. Go out with a notepad and make notes about different events. This could be things in school or at home; they don't have to be serious or big events. Get lots of detailed facts, then practise writing up these different events into informative news articles. To develop your skills in writing to inform, try writing the events up in different forms, such as a speech, a leaflet or a radio broadcast.

1. What type of information dominates in writing to inform?
2. What type of connectives should you be using?
3. What are the two main ways you could organise your writing?

Module 2 | Writing to Explain

The Basics

- Make sure you understand who you're explaining things to and the form of writing that you need to use.
- Writing to explain is all about presenting the facts about something (like writing to inform) and then going into detail about **cause** and **effect**.
- When explaining the cause and effect, you should consider alternatives and try to explain what would happen if something were done differently.
- Plan your ideas carefully, so that you clearly include the stages of giving information and explaining cause and effect. Look at this example structure (each column would be a new section, with each section containing four paragraphs).

Explain Task (example: Explain some of the ways in which people improve their health.)

Information 1 example: exercise more	**Information 2** example: eat healthier meals	**Information 3** example: get enough sleep
Cause 1 join a gym	**Cause 2** cut down on fat and sugar	**Cause 3** go to bed before 10 pm
Alternative cause 1 walk instead of car/bus	**Alternative cause 2** eat your 5 fruit and veg portions every day	**Alternative cause 3** but don't sleep too much
Effect 1 burn fat, strengthen organs	**Effect 2** lower fat, cholesterol, more vitamins	**Effect 3** mentally/physically alert

11

Learn the Key Features of Writing to Explain

- You need to use connectives of cause and effect (for example: as a result, because of this, consequently, due to, therefore, thus).
- You should also use connectives of comparison in order to link your different points together.
- Write in the present tense if you're explaining a current issue (such as the problems affecting teenagers), but the past tense if you're explaining how something happened.
- Usually you'll write in the third person but, if you're asked to explain something about your age-group, you might use the **pronoun** 'we'.

Cause ➤
reason for something happening.

Effect ➤
what happens.

Pronoun ➤
a word that replaces a noun (such as it, she, him).

In pairs, challenge each other to explain a specific process in as much detail as you can. For example, you could explain how a kettle boils water, or how plants grow, or the life cycle of a butterfly. Start by sketching 4-6 pictures of different stages of your process. Then explain each one clearly. The person not explaining should write down questions about anything that is still unclear so you can see how well you've done.

1. What additional information do you focus on that makes explaining different from informing?
2. What type of connectives should you be using?
3. How should you decide what tense to use in writing to explain?

The Basics

- You might be expected to describe something completely imaginary (such as a futuristic world) or a particular scene (for example, a happy memory).
- Develop your descriptions so the reader can really imagine what you're writing about.
- Try to establish settings (and character if necessary) and create a powerful atmosphere.
- Avoid obvious descriptive choices and be creative.
- Try not to keep using general verbs (such as look, go, say); instead, use more specific alternatives (like glance, rush, whisper).
- Remember connectives of time and place so your writing is structured clearly.
- Don't get carried away by your description and forget about your written accuracy.

Descriptive Techniques

- Use a range of descriptive techniques so that your writing is interesting and varied. The reader needs to be able to picture your ideas clearly, but should also find what you've written interesting and original.

12

Descriptive Techniques

- Senses (sight, smell, sound, touch, taste)
- Interesting verbs (doing words), adjectives (describing words) and adverbs (words that describe verbs)
- Simile (a comparison using like or as)
- Sibilance (a series of words containing s sounds)
- Metaphor (an impossible comparison that claims to be true)
- Alliteration (a series of words beginning with the same sound)
- Onomatopoeia (words that sound like the word they refer to)
- Personification (giving nouns human characteristics)

Sentence Structures

- Try to use different sentence structures to create specific effects. For example:

Short, simple sentences	Compound sentences	Complex sentences	Lists
To surprise the reader: *The girl had vanished.*	To create a contrast: *His heart was pounding but his face looked calm.*	To add extra detail: *The rain poured down, hitting the windows like bullets.*	To build up a powerful image: *The gale force winds snapped branches from trees, ripped tiles from roofs, overturned cars and pulled down pylons.*

Genre Specific Vocabulary

- If you're given a particular **genre** to write for, make sure your word choices match. For example, a crime story might use specific words like detective, clue, mystery, perpetrator, victim, investigation and motive.
- Possible genres to think about:

Genre ➤
a style of literature.

Ellipsis ➤
a punctuation mark ... that shows information being missed out (often for dramatic effect).

Make a descriptive writing dice. Print off a cube template from the internet and write different descriptive techniques on each side. Working in a pair, challenge each other to describe something. For each sentence you write, roll the dice and make sure you include the technique that has been rolled. To develop your skills, make another dice that includes the four sentence structures, plus an exclamation mark and an ellipsis; roll both dice together and try to write the technique using the given sentence type or punctuation.

1. When you are writing to describe, what are you trying to give to the reader?
2. What different techniques can you use to build up your descriptions?
3. What effects can you achieve by using different sentence structures?

Module 4 | Writing to Persuade

The Basics

- Make sure you know who you're **persuading** and what form of writing you're using.
- As well as considering the issue from your own point of view, think about the possible views of the people you're addressing as this will help you to make your persuasion more effective.
- Writing to persuade is one-sided (as opposed to two-sided when you write to argue).

Persuade ➤
get someone to think or behave in a certain way.

Mnemonic ➤
something that helps with memory.

Persuasive Techniques

- Revise different persuasive techniques, using the **mnemonic** FORESTRY:

Facts: Support your argument with lots of facts, so you sound like you know what you're talking about.

Opinions: Get your views across in a powerful way; state your opinions as if they are actual facts, rather than writing uncertain phrases like 'I think' or 'maybe'.

Rhetorical questions: These are questions that you ask to get your audience thinking. For example, What can you do to protect the environment?

Emotive and Empathy: Use emotive language to make your readers feel something, such as pride, sympathy or guilt. Empathise with their feelings: by acknowledging their concerns, you can try to win them round.

Statistics: Like using facts, include statistics to make your persuasive points sound researched. This is a test of your writing (not your statistical knowledge) so, as long as they sound realistic, you can make them up.

Triplets: Organise ideas and examples into patterns of three, or triplets, to emphasise a point.

Repetition: Repeat words or phrases in order to highlight a point.

You: When writing to persuade it's much more effective if you address your audience directly ('you', also known as the second person).

Structuring Your Ideas

- Start a new paragraph for each of your persuasive points.
- Use connectives of sequence to make the different parts of a speech clear to the reader (such as, firstly, next, finally).
- Use connectives of comparison to build up your persuasive points (similarly, as well as this, just as).

13

Make persuasive technique cue cards, plus a series of cards with persuasive topics on (such as building a new supermarket, banning homework, or having the next World Cup in England). Working with friends, deal the techniques cards out so everybody has one and then turn over one of the topic cards. Everyone has to come up with a persuasive sentence for the topic, using the technique on their card. If you can't do it, you're out. Keep going round until one person is left; they win that topic card. Then re-deal the techniques cards and turn over a new topic card.

1. **As well as your own opinions, what do you need to consider when trying to persuade someone?**
2. **What mnemonic will help you remember different persuasive techniques?**
3. **What are the different persuasive techniques in the mnemonic?**

Module 5 | Writing to Argue

The Basics

- Remember to ensure that your writing clearly matches the form and audience mentioned in the question.
- Writing to argue is similar to writing to persuade, in that you're presenting your views about an issue. However, in a **balanced argument** you need to present both sides of the issue.
- Use **topic sentences** at the start of your paragraph to help the audience follow your argument.
- Structure your ideas clearly in order to present your argument fully. For example:

Using a short, introductory paragraph, state the issue being debated.

Write a series of paragraphs arguing why you are for or against the issue. Make your views varied and offer clear reasons or evidence.

Then include several paragraphs looking at the alternative views. For each one, unless it has been covered already, offer your counter-argument.

In your final paragraph, present your conclusion and summarise why you are for or against the issue.

Making Use of Persuasive Techniques

- In order to make your argument more effective, use some of the FORESTRY techniques. But don't forget that you're giving both sides of the argument not just your favoured viewpoint:

Facts

Opinions

Rhetorical questions

Emotive and Empathy

Statistics

Triplets

Repetition

You

Balanced argument ➤
presenting both sides of an issue, not just your personal view.

Topic sentence ➤
a sentence that opens a paragraph by summarising what it will be about.

Conclusion ➤
Drawing together different viewpoints and ideas before making a final judgement.

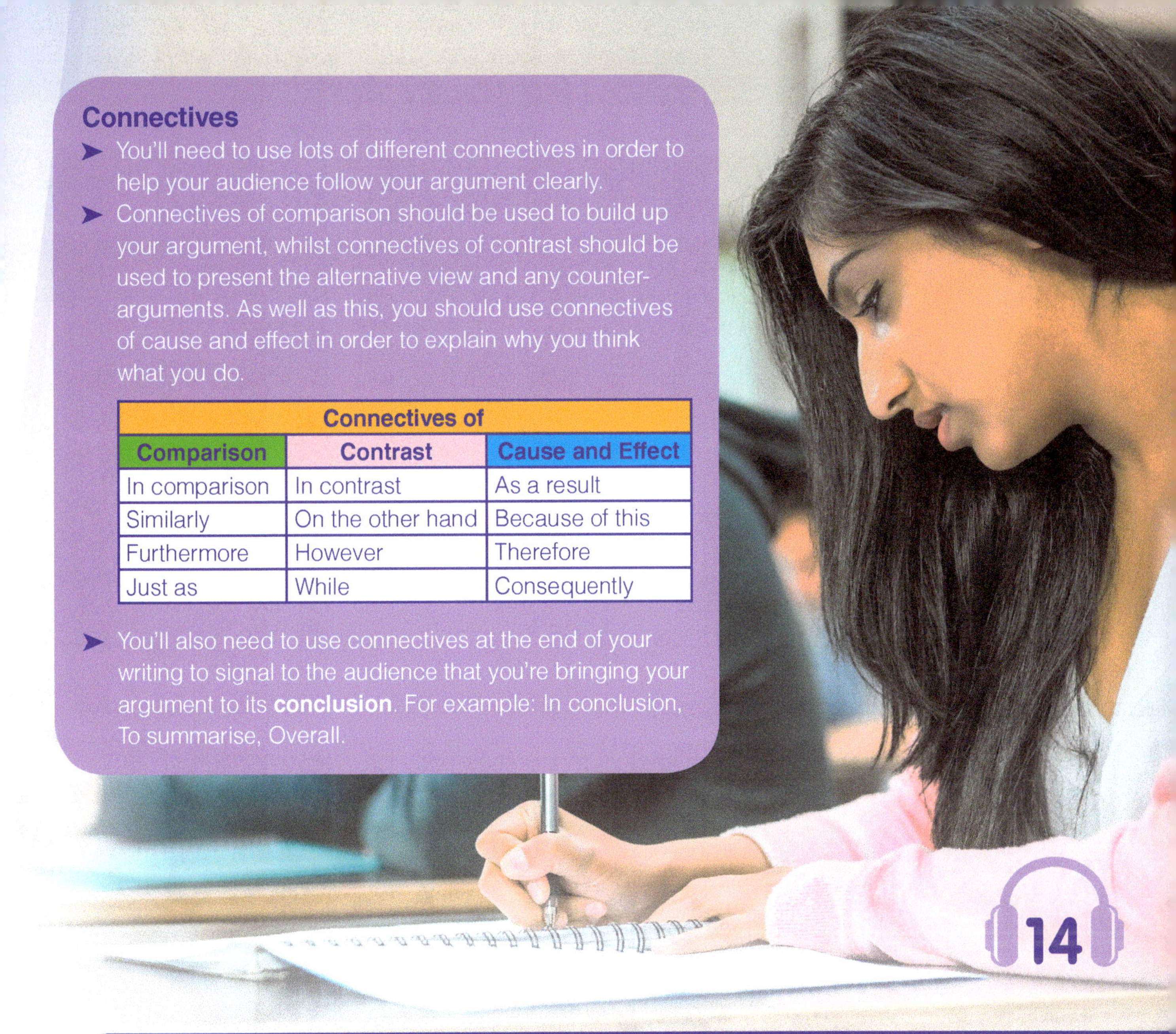

Connectives

- You'll need to use lots of different connectives in order to help your audience follow your argument clearly.
- Connectives of comparison should be used to build up your argument, whilst connectives of contrast should be used to present the alternative view and any counter-arguments. As well as this, you should use connectives of cause and effect in order to explain why you think what you do.

Connectives of		
Comparison	**Contrast**	**Cause and Effect**
In comparison	In contrast	As a result
Similarly	On the other hand	Because of this
Furthermore	However	Therefore
Just as	While	Consequently

- You'll also need to use connectives at the end of your writing to signal to the audience that you're bringing your argument to its **conclusion**. For example: In conclusion, To summarise, Overall.

Make a list of issues or debates that interest you, such as building new facilities for young people, shortening the school holidays, making everyone stay in education until the age of 18. Then create balanced argument posters. Put the points for the issue on the left hand side, and the points against the issue down the right hand side. In the centre, draw two images that summarise the main arguments. To develop your skills, try to put contrasting points opposite each other or add in counter-arguments in a different coloured pen.

1. **How is writing to argue different to writing to persuade?**
2. **What should you include in your final paragraph?**
3. **What different connectives will you need to use?**

Module 6 | Writing to Advise and Instruct

The Basics

- Make sure you know the audience you're instructing or advising, and the form in which you're expected to write.
- Writing to advise is similar to writing to persuade and argue: you're getting across your point of view about what someone should do and trying to get this person to follow it. However, the big difference is your **tone** of voice. You need to be firm but also friendly and supportive in your writing.
- Writing to instruct is also a bit like persuading and arguing, but you're simply telling someone what they need to do so your tone will be quite detached or matter-of-fact. You don't need to give lots of reasons or try to get them thinking for themselves.

Key Features of Writing to Advise and Instruct

- Use the second person (you). This makes the reader feel that you're talking directly to them about something that they need help with.
- Give clear orders (also called imperatives). These will contain the instructions or advice that you want to pass on to your reader. When advising, to keep your orders sounding friendly, begin them with a friendly, empathising phrase, for example: *Although it might be hard at first, you must speak to your parents about how you feel.*
- Learning a variety of **modal verbs** can help with your advice and instruction:

Modal Verb	Used in a sentence to advise	Used in a sentence to instruct
Could	*You could speak to a friend.*	*You could use scissors or a knife to cut the card.*
Must	*You must prove to the people at work that you know what you are talking about.*	*You must unplug the electrical appliance before you begin.*
Need	*You need to build up your self-confidence.*	*You need to screw the legs of the stand into the base.*
Should	*You should ignore what she is saying about you and get on with your life.*	*You should now replace the casing before continuing.*

- When advising, use some of the FORESTRY persuasive techniques, such as: opinions, rhetorical questions, empathy, triplets, and repetition. These will make your audience think you're right, and therefore make them more likely to follow your advice.
- When instructing, you might also explain why something needs to be done in the way you have said. This could be done using connectives of cause and effect, for example: This is due to, Because. This will reassure people that you're an expert in what you are writing about.

15

Structuring Your Writing

- You need to order your ideas logically in the planning stage and then, when writing, use lots of connectives of sequence. This is so the reader can clearly follow what they need to do.
- When instructing, your connectives can be quite mechanical (firstly, secondly, next, finally).
- When advising, you are trying to appear more friendly, so your connectives should be more varied (e.g. to begin with, after this, once this has been achieved).

Tone ➤
the emotion in writing or speech.

Modal verb ➤
a word that is added to another verb to suggest necessity or choice (should, would, could).

Working with a friend, practise using orders and connectives to instruct. Set each other a task (such as: Instruct me how to make a cup of tea) and write your responses. Then follow each other's instructions and see if they work. Discuss where the instructions were clear and where they needed improving. Then practise using tone and connectives to advise each other how to cope with all your GCSE homework and revision. Prepare short speeches and perform them to each other; as your friend speaks, note down all the useful connectives and all the friendly, supportive phrases that they use.

1. **Why are connectives important in writing to advise and instruct?**
2. **What are modal verbs and why are they useful in this type of writing?**
3. **Why is tone important in writing to advise?**

Module 7 | Spelling Rules and Tips

Why Spelling is Important

- All of your exams will contain a mark for your written accuracy, especially when your writing skills are being tested. If you struggle with your spelling, you should try to improve it by getting in the habit of reading a lot and trying different online tests.
- Don't make mistakes spelling words that are already spelled for you on the exam paper.
- If time is short before your exams, you could focus on improving the key areas covered on these pages.

Plural ➤
when there is more than one of something

Abbreviation ➤
shortening of words

Preposition ➤
a word to show the position of things in terms of time or place

Subject Specific Words

- Make sure you have learned the sort of words that you will use regularly in your English exams. For example:

Useful Words for Analysis Questions

- The title and author of the texts you have revised
- simile, metaphor, personification
- verb, noun, adjective, adverb
- suggest, convey, imply
- character, setting, atmosphere
- website, autobiography, article
- poem, novel, fiction, non-fiction
- author, writer, poet
- paragraph, stanza, sentence, quotation
- headline, photograph, interview

Useful Words for Writing Tasks

- dear, faithfully, sincerely
- firstly, addition, conclusion
- question, answer, consider
- result, effect, consequence
- important, significant, necessary
- business, government, school, council
- yesterday, morning, afternoon, evening, night

Homophones

➤ Homophones are words that sound the same but have different meanings and spellings. Try to remember the spellings of key homophones so you don't make silly mistakes.

buy (to purchase)	by (a preposition meaning near or on)	bye (abbreviation of goodbye)
there (place)	their (ownership)	they're (abbreviation of they are)
too (suggesting excess)	two (a number)	to (a preposition of direction)
write (an action)	right (a direction, or being correct)	
where (place)	wear (to put on)	
your (ownership)	you're (abbreviation of you are)	

Word Endings

➤ Students also make mistakes with the endings of words. Over the next few weeks or months, when you're reading, look out for the following things about word endings:

- ➤ Do nouns end in -s or -es for their **plural**? (car = cars; box = boxes) Nouns ending with a -y become -ies for their plural. (baby = babies)
- ➤ When verbs change tense, which words just add -ing or -ed, and which words also double the last consonant? (play = playing/played; scan = scanning/scanned)
- ➤ Which verbs change completely in the past tense? (run = ran; say = said)
- ➤ Learn familiar word endings that appear a lot. For example: -tion (attention, motion); -ble (able, horrible); -ous (gorgeous, adventurous).

16

Make a word wheel of subject specific words that you're struggling with. Give it to a friend and ask them to spin it and test you. To develop your skills, play lots of word games in magazines and online, such as 'Scrabble' or 'Words With Friends'.

1. How many words can you list that end -tion?
2. What are the differences in meaning between there, their, and they're?
3. What other homophones do you know and what are their different meanings?

Sentences

- You should use a variety of sentence structures in your writing. This will show you have a good level of literacy, as well as bringing variety to your work and allowing you to use sentences to achieve different effects.
- In order to structure a range of sentences, you need to understand the three basic types.

- Simple sentences contain one verb and one idea (The old house was deserted.)
- Compound sentences are two simple sentences joined by a **conjunction** (The old house was deserted and its windows were all broken.)
- Complex sentences have a **main clause** and a **subordinate clause**, separated by a comma (The old house was deserted, its smashed windows revealing only darkness within.)
- Complex sentences are the main type of sentence you should be using as they allow you to present your ideas in detail. The main clause should always make sense on its own, but the subordinate clause will not make sense on its own.
- The subordinate clause can also be put in different positions to add further variety to your writing: before the main clause (Its smashed windows revealing only darkness within, the old house was deserted.); in the middle of the main clause (The old house, its smashed windows revealing only darkness within, was deserted.); after the main clause (The old house was deserted, its smashed windows revealing only darkness within). Notice that you need two commas if you place the subordinate clause in the middle of the main clause.

Commas

- As well as using commas to separate the main and subordinate clauses in a complex sentence, you should also remember to use commas between items in a list.
- You can choose whether your last item has a comma or not as there is no set rule. For example:
  - I bought apples, oranges, pears, and lemons.
  - I bought books, sweets, toys and comics.

Conjunction ➤ a joining word (for example: and, but, whilst).

Main clause ➤ the main idea in a sentence (it should always make sense on its own).

Subordinate clause ➤ additional information in a sentence.

Proper noun ➤ a noun that has a specific name or title and a capital letter.

17

Capital Letters

- Students often make careless mistakes with capital letters.
- You need them at the start of a sentence.
- If the letter i is being used as a pronoun it should be capitalised. For example: I, I've, I'd.
- You need them for **proper nouns**: the *names* of people, establishments, towns and countries, etc. For example: Mike, West Lodge School, Northampton, Ireland.

Apostrophes

The Different Uses of Apostrophes

Abbreviation
Add an apostrophe where two words have been joined and letters missed out (could have > could've; he is > he's).

Single ownership
Just add 's (the dog's bone; Jack's coat).

Ownership when the person's name ends with an -s
Still add 's (Jess's bag; Mr Jones's house). However, if their name ends with an -iz sound, just add the apostrophe (Mrs Bridges' car).

When something is owned by a group
Just add the apostrophe (the two dogs' bone; the boys' coats).

Tenses

- When you're writing, you need to choose a tense that matches your purpose and form. For example, if you're describing something that has happened it needs to be in the past tense, or if you're inviting people to a forthcoming event you would need to use the future tense, but if you're writing about what something is currently like you would use the present tense.
- You need to make sure that your tense choices are consistent and correct, otherwise your work will be confusing to read.

Working with a partner, each find a paragraph in a book or magazine. Copy it out but remove all the punctuation and capital letters. Swap your incorrect versions and see if you can correct all the grammar and punctuation errors. To develop each other's skills, you could add in some incorrect spellings as well.

1. **What are the three main types of sentences?**
2. **When should you use capital letters?**
3. **What are the two main uses of an apostrophe?**

Planning

- Once you've read the question and understood your purpose, audience and form, you should plan your response.
- Using whatever method you prefer, come up with different ideas for the content of your task.
- You could also note any specific techniques that you might use to convey different bits of your content.

Structuring

- When you've got your ideas noted down, you should read them through and number them in a logical order.
- You can treat each number as a paragraph and this will ensure that your ideas flow sensibly and allow you to build your writing up.

Example of a Student's Plan

Write a speech persuading your peers to recycle.

1) Open with a brief introduction to the speech – acknowledge audience. Use you. Include facts. Rhetorical question.

2) Explain problems with environment linked to lack of recycling – too many rubbish dumps, burning rubbish leads to harmful gases in atmosphere. Emotive language about destroying the planet. Rhetorical question.

3) How recycling helps – not using up the world's resources. Statistic about trees being cut down for paper.

4) Use the recycling bins at school – paper in class; food packaging at break and lunch. Pattern of three to emphasise using recycling bins.

5) Recycle at home – food waste, packaging, etc. Make it sound easy. Empathise that it may seem a hassle. Use imperative.

6) Encourage others – convince your mates to use the correct bins, get your parents to join in. Imperatives and repetition about convincing others. Strong, memorable ending.

18

Developing

- Make sure that each paragraph is fully developed.
- Don't just move onto a new paragraph each time you've written an idea. Think about whether you can build on it or emphasise it. For example, this could be done through lots of detailed imagery (in descriptive writing), or by giving examples and evidence to support your ideas (in writing to explain), etc.
- Developing your work allows you to show off your skills as a writer, giving you the room to use a range of language and sentence structures.

Inform
- Facts and statistics
- Connectives of time and place
- Avoid feelings and opinions
- Positive and negative language
- Third person
- Thematic or chronological structure

Explain
- Present tense for current issues
- Facts
- Past tense for things that have happened
- Connectives of cause and effect
- Information presented in logical stages

Describe
- Lots of detail to help the reader picture your ideas
- Atmosphere, setting and character
- Varied vocabulary and descriptive techniques
- Range of sentence structures
- Connectives of time and place

Argue
- Connectives of comparison, contrast, and cause and effect
- Persuasive techniques
- Conclusion
- Topic sentences
- Clear opinion but both sides of the issue presented

Persuade
- Rhetorical questions
- Opinions
- Repetition
- You
- Facts
- Statistics
- Triplets
- Emotive language and empathy

Advise and Instruct
- Instruct people what they must do; advise what they should do
- Give orders
- Tone of voice
- Modal verbs
- Connectives of sequence

Be sure of your purpose, audience and form.

Remember to check spelling, punctuation, and grammar.

1. Imagine a celebrity has visited your school. Write an article for your local newspaper about the event. Include:
   - who the celebrity was and why they were visiting the school
   - the different things that happened during the visit
   - how students and staff felt about the celebrity's visit.

2. Write the text for a leaflet to be handed out to GCSE students in your year, explaining why the exams period can be stressful and ways they can cope. Include:
   - reasons why the exam period is stressful
   - suggestions for coping
   - explanations of why these coping strategies can help.

3. You are entering a competition in a creative writing magazine. Write a description inspired by this photograph:

4. Write the text for a speech to be given to school governors, arguing the pros and cons of school uniform. Include:
   - a balanced argument
   - a clear conclusion.

5. Write a letter to your local MP about why more money should be spent on providing leisure facilities exclusively for young people. Include:
   - what leisure facilities young people would find beneficial
   - why government and local councils should spend money on these facilities.

6. Write an article for a teenage magazine about how to cope with starting secondary school. Include:
   - advice on making a good impression
   - advice on making friends
   - advice on coping with a new environment and a new timetable.

7. Write the text for a leaflet aimed at pensioners who have bought their first laptop. Your leaflet should help people understand how to search the internet and send emails. Include:
   - instructions for getting online with their new laptop
   - instructions about how to search the internet
   - instructions on sending email.

Re-Reading Poems

- You will have studied a selection of poetry in class, such as Love and Relationships, Power and Conflict, or Time and Place. Make sure you have read the poems several times before going into the exam.

Grouping Poems Together by Theme

- To help you revise, think about the ways in which some of your poems are similar.
- For example, if you're studying Love and Relationships, some of the poems might be about romantic love, family relationships, sexual desire, or unrequited love.
- Similarly, if you're studying Power and Conflict, you might have themes of personal disagreements, individuals in a war, the effects of war, or the causes of conflict.
- Some poems will go into more than one group.
- When you've grouped your poems, think about which lines are particularly good at conveying the poets' messages.

Pattern of three ➤
three related ideas in a list.

Enjambment ➤
creating a dramatic pause by carrying a sentence across two lines or stanzas of poetry.

Grouping Poems Together by Technique

- Another way to revise your poems is to group them by technique.
- Which ones use similes in an effective way, or create surprising images, or convey their ideas through metaphor, or use repetition to highlight their viewpoint?
- This will give you a deeper understanding of how the poets are using language and structure in their work.
- As well as identifying different techniques, you need to think about how they help to get across a poet's ideas. Are they creating a memorable image, or helping the reader to imagine something, or highlighting important words, or emphasising a key point, or building up an idea?

19

Learn Your Techniques

- When you look at lines of poetry that get across a poet's ideas, you need to be able to comment on the language and structure that they are using.
- Make sure that you know the following language techniques:

Language Techniques	
Adjective	a word that describes a noun or object.
Adverb	a word that describes a verb.
Alliteration	repeating the same sound at the start of a series of words.
Assonance	repeating vowel sounds within a series of words.
Contrast	using two opposite ideas or images.
Metaphor	a comparison that is impossible but is written as if true (rather than 'like').
Onomatopoeia	words that sound like the word they refer to.
Personification	writing about an object as if it has human qualities.
Simile	a comparison that uses 'like' or 'as'.
Symbolism	an image that represents another meaning (e.g. red can symbolise love or danger).
Verb	a word that conveys an action.

- You should also learn to identify different features of structure.

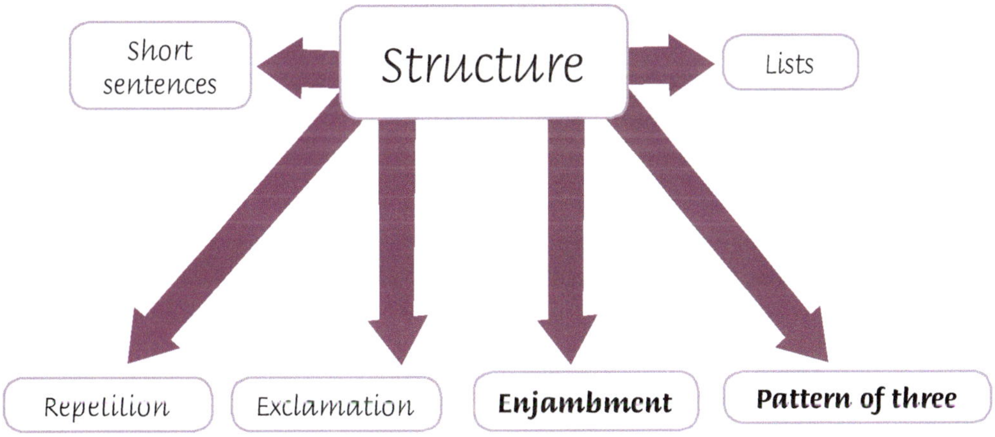

On a sheet of A3 paper, make a table that explores your selection of poetry. Write the titles in the left-hand column, then different themes and techniques along the top. Work through each poem, ticking which themes and techniques appear. To develop your skills, make the boxes on your table big enough to add key quotations as evidence.

1. What are the definitions of verb, adjective, and adverb?
2. What is the difference between a simile and a metaphor?
3. What different structural techniques can a poet use to emphasise ideas?

First Impressions: Themes

- When you're given an unseen poem to analyse, start by reading it through and deciding, simply, what the poem is about.
- Think also about the speaker's viewpoint (this could be the poet's voice, or they could be taking on the narrative voice of a character).
- Once you've decided on the poem's themes and ideas, you're in a position to explain how the poet gets this across to the reader through language, **form** and structure.

TIFS

- A good way to analyse a poem, and help you structure your response, is to think about TIFS: themes, imagery, form, structure.

Horned Poppy

by *Vicki Feaver*

Frailest of flowers, armoured to survive
at the edge of the sea: leaves
tough as holly, hugging the stem
like spiked cuffs; the buds protected
by a prickly sheath; the petals furled
like yellow parachute silk, opening to expose,
at its radiant heart, the threads
of stamens, pollen's loose dust.
It blooms for at the most an hour;
torn apart by the elements it loves.
And then the pistil grows:
a live bootlace, a fuse
of multiplying cells – reaching out
to feel between the shingle's
sharp-edged flints for a moist bed
to lay its seed; or in my kitchen,
drying in the heat, a long thin hand
summoning a salt gale, a tide to roll in
over the flat land, roaring
through the open door.

*stamen / pistil = the reproductive organs of a flower
*shingle = the small pebbles on a beach

In response to the poem opposite, a student might write:

Themes

- Nature. The poet seems impressed by the flower but also sorry for it. She may be a bit guilty for taking it home (away from its natural environment).

Imagery

- Contrasting adjectives (frailest/armoured) – feels sorry for it, but is also impressed.
- Alliteration (frailest of flowers) – highlights the flower's vulnerability.
- Contrasting verbs (blooms / torn apart) – it's beautiful but quickly destroyed.
- Similes (tough as holly / like spike cuffs) to explore the impressive, strong side.
- Simile (like silk) to explore the gentle side.
- Metaphor (radiant heart) – she thinks it's beautiful/ impressive.
- Metaphor (live bootlace) – helps us imagine the pistil growing; she's fascinated by its life-cycle.
- Personification (long thin hand) – makes it seem old/weak/ desperate to suggest maybe she shouldn't have taken it home.

Form

- The **meter** isn't uniform which makes the poem look a bit ragged. This lack of uniformity can also be seen in the blank verse and enjambment. This could represent the wild, unprotected environment that the poppy grows in (which impresses the poet but also makes her sorry for the poppy, as it's eventually 'torn apart by the elements').

Structure

- Quite short, two-line sentence in the middle of the poem – emphasises the poet's main feelings of admiration and sadness.
- Lists of descriptions – builds up a detailed picture of the flower.
- Lots of short **clauses** in the first half of the poem – creates a series of dramatic pauses that suggest something (bad) is going to happen.

Form ➤ the type of a poem, such as a sonnet or a ballad. This includes the shape of a poem: the number of stanzas, the number of lines in those stanzas (for example, two lines = a couplet; four lines = a quatrain), whether there is a rhyme scheme, whether there is a clear meter, etc.

Meter ➤ the number of syllables/beats per line.

Clauses ➤ the parts of a sentence, each separated by punctuation.

20

Choose any poem (from the internet, or a section of the poetry anthology that you haven't studied). Stick it onto the middle of a sheet of A3 paper. Using different colours for the four areas of TIFS, annotate the things you notice about the poem.

1. What does TIFS stand for?
2. Every time you identify a feature of language or structure, what do you need to link it to?
3. What is form?

Sticking With TIFS

- Analysing an unseen poem from the literary heritage may seem difficult because the language is more old-fashioned. However, just continue to explore themes, imagery, form, and structure.
- You could get a question like this: How does Wordsworth present the city of London in his poem?

Composed upon Westminster Bridge, September 3, 1802
by *William Wordsworth*

Earth has not anything to show more fair:
Dull would he be of soul who could pass by
A sight so touching in its majesty:
This City now doth, like a garment, wear
The beauty of the morning; silent, bare,
Ships, towers, domes, theatres, and temples lie
Open unto the fields, and to the sky;
All bright and glittering in the smokeless air.
Never did sun more beautifully steep
In his first splendour, valley, rock, or hill;
Ne'er saw I, never felt, a calm so deep!
The river glideth at his own sweet will:
Dear God! the very houses seem asleep;
And all that mighty heart is lying still!

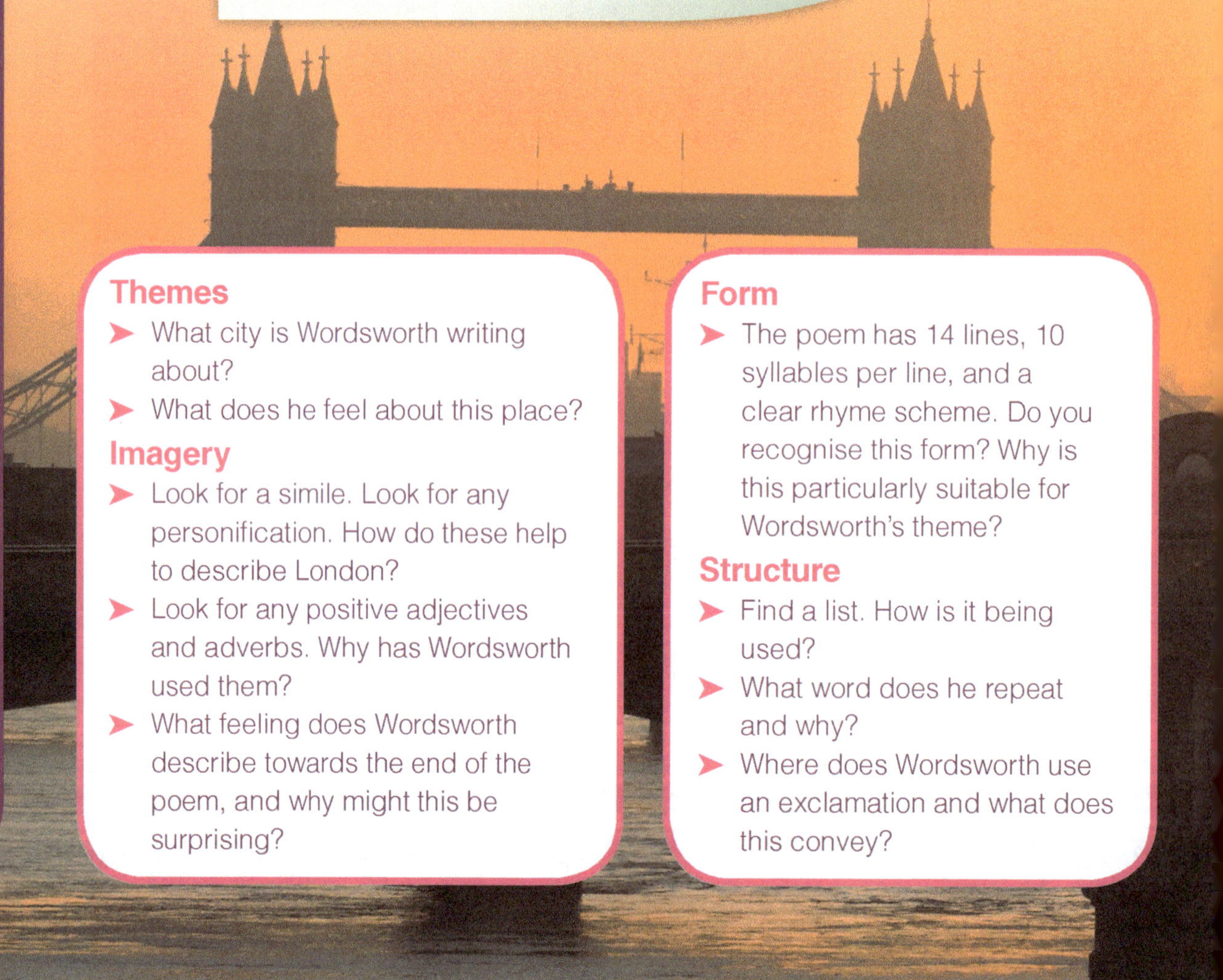

Themes

- What city is Wordsworth writing about?
- What does he feel about this place?

Imagery

- Look for a simile. Look for any personification. How do these help to describe London?
- Look for any positive adjectives and adverbs. Why has Wordsworth used them?
- What feeling does Wordsworth describe towards the end of the poem, and why might this be surprising?

Form

- The poem has 14 lines, 10 syllables per line, and a clear rhyme scheme. Do you recognise this form? Why is this particularly suitable for Wordsworth's theme?

Structure

- Find a list. How is it being used?
- What word does he repeat and why?
- Where does Wordsworth use an exclamation and what does this convey?

Writing Your Analysis

- Start with a simple introduction that states the themes you've identified. For example:
  Wordsworth is describing how beautiful and impressive the city of London is at sunrise.
- Explain how these themes are conveyed through imagery. For example:
  One way in which Wordsworth conveys the beauty of London is through a combination of personification and simile, 'This City now doth like a garment wear / The beauty of the morning'. The image of clothes and the ***abstract noun*** *'beauty' suggests that London looks perfectly presented. Describing the city as a person is quite striking, which helps to show the impact that the city has had on the writer.*
  Wordsworth also uses positive adjectives and adverbs to emphasise his love of London, 'fair... bright and glittering... beautifully'. These words all link to beauty, as if he sees the city as an attractive woman. The use of 'bright and glittering' links to richness (perhaps like a woman's jewellery), which suggest that Wordsworth values the city highly.
- Comment on the relevance of the form used by the poet. For example:
  Wordsworth's choice of a sonnet is significant. He wants to convey his love of London, so he has chosen a form of love poetry. With its 14 lines, 10 syllables per line, and rhyme scheme, this is also a tightly constructed form, which could reflect how London is a packed, man-made city rather than a piece of nature.
- Explore how the poet has used structure. For example:
  Wordsworth uses a list form to describe London, 'Ships, towers, domes, theatres, and temples'. This builds up our impression of the city so we can share Wordsworth's feelings. He includes very different shapes and places so we can visualise how diverse it is.
  He continues to show how impressed he is by the use of an exclamation, 'Dear God!'. Coupled with the biblical language, this suggests that he is almost shocked by how wonderful the city is, but also, through the link to prayer, that he sees it as a gift from God.

21

Abstract noun ➤
an idea or feeling (like love, happiness, or time); unlike a regular noun, it cannot be held or touched.

Practise your poetry techniques. Make two cardboard dice and write different techniques of language and structure on their faces. Throw the dice and try to write a description of something in your room using the two techniques that come up.

1. What four things should you focus on when analysing an unseen poem?
2. What three things should you try to do in each paragraph of your analysis?
3. What is a sonnet?

Module 4 | Comparing Modern Unseen Poetry

Getting Started

- When comparing unseen poetry, you need to read the poems individually and think about TIFS: themes, imagery, form, and structure. Underline any particular phrases or techniques that stand out to you.
- You then need to find some points of comparison.

Ideas for Comparison

- The exam question may state a theme, such as nature or friendship, but you still need to find three or four ideas within that. For example, one idea might be that the poets are fascinated by nature, and another that nature can be frightening, etc. Alternatively, you might have two poets who have different ideas about friendship: one may explore friendship formed as a child, while the other explores an adult friendship; one may conclude that friends are the most important thing, whilst the other may believe family comes first.
- Each of your ideas will allow you to build up a paragraph of comparison.

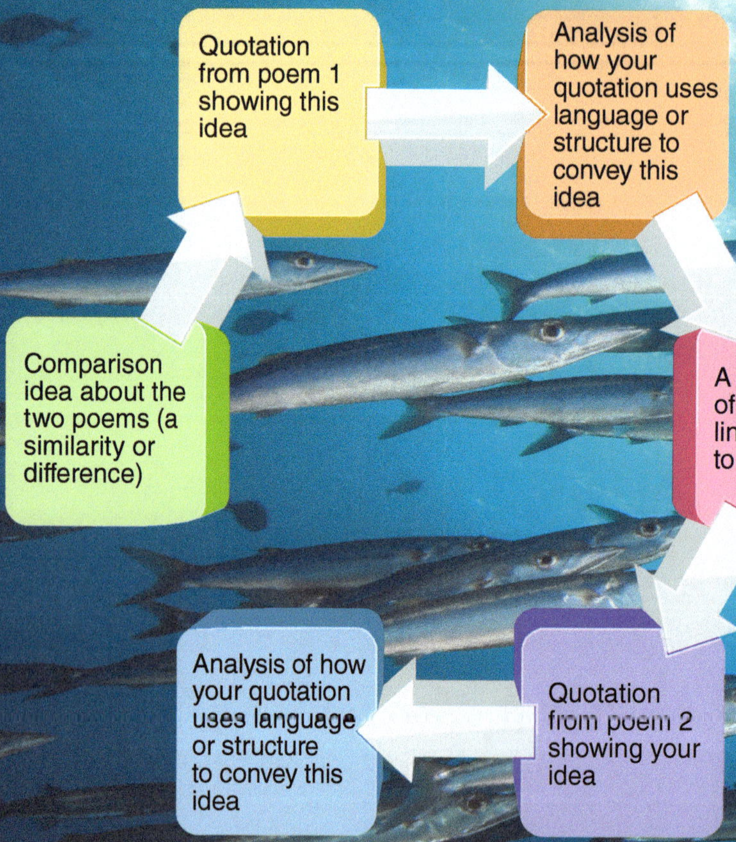

Imperative ➤
an order.

Colloquialism ➤
an everyday or slang phrase.

Superlative adjective ➤
an adjective that describes the most something can be (smallest).

22

Exploring Two Poems

- Look at these two short poems. They are both about sea life, but what other comparison ideas could you come up with? How could you analyse the ways in which language and structure are used to show these ideas?

Fish

by Mary Ann Hoberman

Look at them flit
Lickety-split
Wiggling
Swiggling
Swerving
Curving
Hurrying
Scurrying
Chasing
Racing
Whizzing
Whisking
Flying
Frisking
Tearing around
With a leap and a bound
But none of them making the tiniest
tiniest
tiniest
tiniest
tiniest
Sound

A Jelly-Fish

by *Marianne Moore*

Visible, invisible,
a fluctuating charm
an amber-tinctured amethyst
inhabits it, your arm
approaches and it opens
and it closes; you had meant
to catch it and it quivers;
you abandon your intent.

- Both are fascinated by the creatures. Moore shows this through contrast and metaphor, whilst Hoberman uses an **imperative** and a **colloquialism** about their speed.
- Both describe how the sea life moves. Moore uses a verb and metaphor, whilst Hoberman uses a list of rhyming verbs.
- The jellyfish is ultimately a bit scary, whilst the fish seem small and vulnerable. Moore uses a verb and a short clause for emphasis, whilst Hoberman uses repetition of a **superlative adjective**.
- Both use form to reflect their subject. Moore's poem is only eight lines long with similar length lines, making it look small and compact like the jellyfish. Hoberman's use of single word lines represents individual fish, whilst the indented lines at the end suggest the fish darting away from her or getting quieter.

Find two poems that are on a similar theme. Decide what the two poems are about. Cut them up and stick key lines for comparison next to each other. Make a set of similarities and a set of differences. Use a highlighter to identify techniques of language and structure.

1. **What four things do you need to focus on when exploring an unseen poem?**
2. **What do you need to use to link your ideas?**
3. **What is a colloquialism?**

Remembering the Skills You've Revised

- If you have to compare a modern poem with a poem from the literary heritage, remember to use TIFS to help you deconstruct the poems' meanings.

Sibilance ➤ repeated use of 's' sounds.

23

Practising Your Skills

- Thinking TIFS, come up with a series of comparisons about the two poems below. Make sure you can back up your ideas with quotations and concise, specific analysis.

You

by *Carol Ann Duffy*

Uninvited, the thought of you stayed too late in my head.
so I went to bed, dreaming you hard, hard, woke with your name,
like tears, soft, salt, on my lips, the sound of its bright syllables
like a charm, like a spell.

Falling in love
is glamorous hell: the crouched, parched heart
like a tiger, ready to kill; a flame's fierce licks under the skin.
into my life, larger than life, you strolled in.

I hid in my ordinary days, in the long grass of routine,
in my camouflage rooms. You sprawled in my gaze,
staring back from anyone's face, from the shape of a cloud,
from the pining, earth-struck moon which gapes at me

as I open the bedroom door. The curtains stir. There you are
on the bed, like gift, like a touchable dream.

Sonnet 42

by *William Shakespeare*

That thou hast her, it is not all my grief,
And yet it may be said I loved her dearly;
That she hath thee, is of my wailing chief,
A loss in love that touches me more nearly.
Loving offenders, thus I will excuse ye:
Thou dost love her, because thou knowst I love her;
And for my sake even so doth she abuse me,
Suffering my friend for my sake to approve her.
If I lose thee, my loss is my love's gain,
And losing her, my friend hath found that loss;
Both find each other, and I lose both twain,
And both for my sake lay on me this cross:
  But here's the joy; my friend and I are one;
  Sweet flattery! then she loves but me alone.

Comparison	Imagery / Form / Structure	Analysis
Both are about love	Sonnet form	Traditional form of love poetry. Duffy's lines don't have the usual ten syllables, perhaps to show that this love isn't usual.
Both describe passion	Metaphor and simile in the first stanza of *You*. Shakespeare's use of the adverb 'dearly'.	Both use language to emphasise their feelings.
One addresses a lover, the other addresses the man who took his lover.	Repetition of the pronoun 'you', and metaphor in stanza 3. Repetition of 'thou', and metaphor in line 12.	Duffy's speaker can't get the lover out of her head, whilst Shakespeare focuses more on the man who took his lover: he is more concerned at losing his friend.
Duffy's poem has a happy outcome, but Shakespeare's doesn't.	Similes in the last stanza of *You*. Repetition of loss, but some false hope in the final couplet.	In Duffy's poem, the speaker feels like love is an unbelievable gift, whereas Shakespeare feels he's lost everything. He tries to convince himself that as he and his friend are so similar, the woman must also still love him.

Practising Writing Your Analysis

➤ A written comparison of the two poems opposite might look like this:

Both poets explore the pain of love. Duffy describes love as a 'parched heart / like a tiger ready to kill; a flame's fierce licks under the skin'. The simile and metaphor both contain images of sickness (like a fever) and danger. Alliteration emphasises the image of burning, as if the heat that is traditionally linked to passion is too much, whilst the sibilance in the last clause creates a hiss like a danger warning. In comparison, Shakespeare refers to 'my grief... my wailing'. The use of the abstract noun suggests the pain is almost like someone has died, whilst the verb makes him sound like a child that is inconsolable.

Can you find...?

1. Clear point of comparison
2. Reference to the first poem and a quotation
3. Analysis of how the quotation shows the point
4. Further development of analysis
5. Connective of comparison and link to second poem
6. Quotation from second poem
7. Analysis of how the quotation shows the point

Working with a friend, pick two similar poems each. Cut out pairs of lines that could be compared and paperclip them together. Swap them with each other and see if you can tell your friend how the two poets are using language and structure.

1. **Why might it be easier to start by exploring the modern poem?**
2. **What should you always use to link your points about two different poems?**
3. **What is sibilance?**

Poetry | Mind Map

Cluster poetry

- Learn your techniques of language.
- Practise grouping your poems by theme.
- Re-read your poems several times.
- Practise grouping your poems by technique.
- Learn your techniques of structure.

Unseen poetry

- Refer to the effects of specific techniques.
- Support your ideas with quotations and analysis.
- Read the poem carefully whilst underlining parts that stand out.
- TIFS: Theme, Imagery, Form, Structure
- Think about what the poem is about and the speaker's viewpoint.

Comparing poems

- Read the poems carefully.
- Come up with three or four points of comparison.
- Link your poems with connectives of comparison.
- State your idea, support it with a quotation, analyse how language or structure shows your idea.
- Alternate your ideas between the two poems (not half the essay on one poem, then half on the other).
- Read the question thoroughly so you know the focus for comparison.

Daughter

There is one grief worse than any other.

When your small feverish throat clogged,
and quit
I knelt beside the chair on the green rug
and shook you and shook you,
but the only sound was mine shouting you back,
the delicate curls at your temples,
the blue wool blanket,
your face blue,
your jaw clamped against remedy—

how could I put a knife to that white neck?
With you in my lap,
my hands fluttering like flags,
I bend instead over your dead weight
to administer a kiss so urgent, so ruthless,
pumping breath into your stilled body,
counting out the rhythm for how long until
the second birth, the second cry
oh Jesus that sudden noisy musical inhalation
that leaves me stunned
by your survival.

Her First Week

She was so small I would scan the crib a half-second
to find her, face-down in a corner, limp
as something gently flung down, or fallen
from some sky an inch above the mattress. I would
tuck her arm along her side
and slowly turn her over. She would tumble
over part by part, like a load
of damp laundry, in the dryer, I'd slip
a hand in, under her neck,
slide the other under her back,
and evenly lift her up. Her little bottom
sat in my palm, her chest contained
the puckered, moire sacs, and her neck -
I was afraid of her neck, once I almost
thought I heard it quietly snap,
I looked at her and she swivelled her slate
eyes and looked at me. It was in
my care, the creature of her spine, like the first
chordate, as if the history
of the vertebrate had been placed in my hands.

Every time I checked, she was still
with us - someday, there would be a human
race. I could not see it in her eyes,
but when I fed her, gathered her
like a loose bouquet to my side and offered
the breast, greyish-white, and struck with
minuscule scars like creeks in sunlight, I
felt she was serious, I believed she was willing to stay.

1. Cluster Poetry.
   Choose two poems from your anthology and compare how they present one of the following themes:
   a) A relationship
   b) Conflict
   c) Nature
   d) Age
2. Single Unseen Analysis.
   In 'Daughter', by Ellen Bryant Voigt, the poet's child almost chokes to death. How does the poet convey her feelings about her daughter?
3. Compare 'Daughter' by Ellen Bryant Voigt with 'Her First Week' by Sharon Olds. How do the two poets convey the thoughts and feelings of mothers with young children?

First Impressions

➤ Start by revising who your key characters are and their **characteristics** at the start of the play. For example:

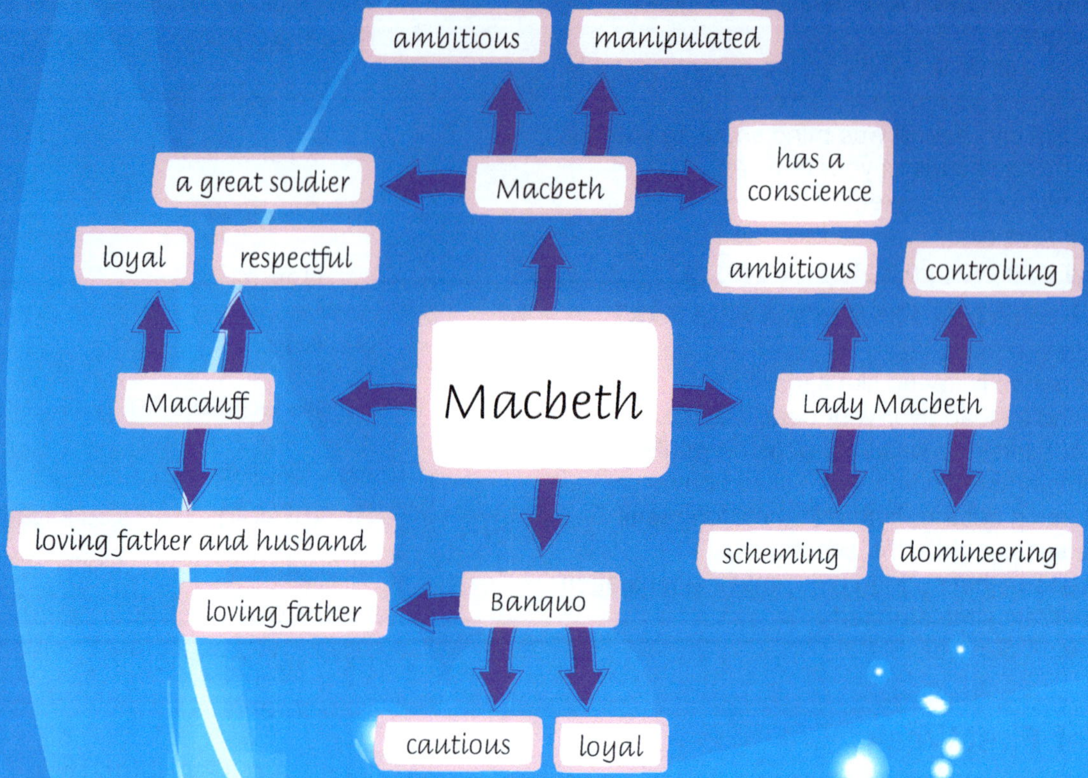

First Impressions: Evidence

➤ For all your ideas, you need to think about how Shakespeare shows this.

➤ You don't need to learn big chunks of the play, but try to remember key events and learn some key words. For example:

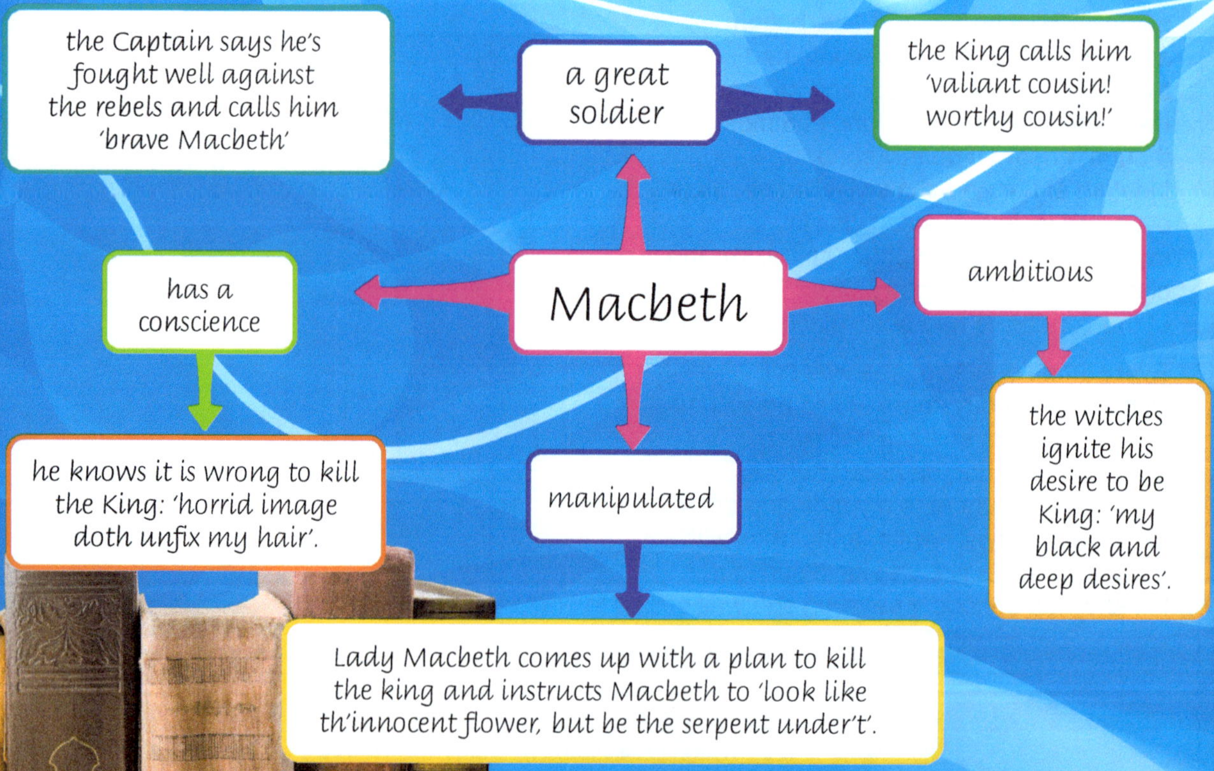

Development

- Once you have established what your character is like at the start of the play, you need to think about how your character is developed.
- Does Shakespeare give more examples of a specific characteristic?
- Does Shakespeare change the character in any way?
- Try to link your ideas to specific events in the play and key words or phrases from the text. For example:

Benedick

In *Much Ado About Nothing*, Benedick begins the play as comical, rude, unromantic and disliking Beatrice. Later he becomes romantic ('I have railed so long against marriage: but does not the appetite alter?'), in love with Beatrice ('I do with an eye of love requite her'; marrying her) and heroic (agreeing to a duel with Claudio for Beatrice).

Lord Capulet

At the start of *Romeo and Juliet*, Lord Capulet is shown to be powerful and aggressive, but a loving father. However, later on he tries to calm the Capulet/Montague feud (ordering Tybalt to ignore Romeo at the party). He becomes cruel to Juliet ('Hang! Beg! Starve! Die in the streets!'), but he makes friends with the Montagues at the end ('Brother Montague, give me thy hand').

Characteristics ➤ what a person is like (their behaviour, thoughts, and attitudes).

24

Stick two pieces of A3 paper together to create a long sheet of paper. Sketch each of your characters down the left-hand side. Then create a timeline for each character, sketching key events, including key quotations, and noting how the characters change. Add a sketch on the far-right of your sheet, showing how the characters end the play (such as happily married or dead).

1. What two things should you consider about your main characters?
2. Pick who you think is the most important character in your play; what are they like at the start?
3. How do they develop and how does the play show you this?

Identifying Themes

- Start by deciding on four or five key themes that appear in the play you've studied. For example:

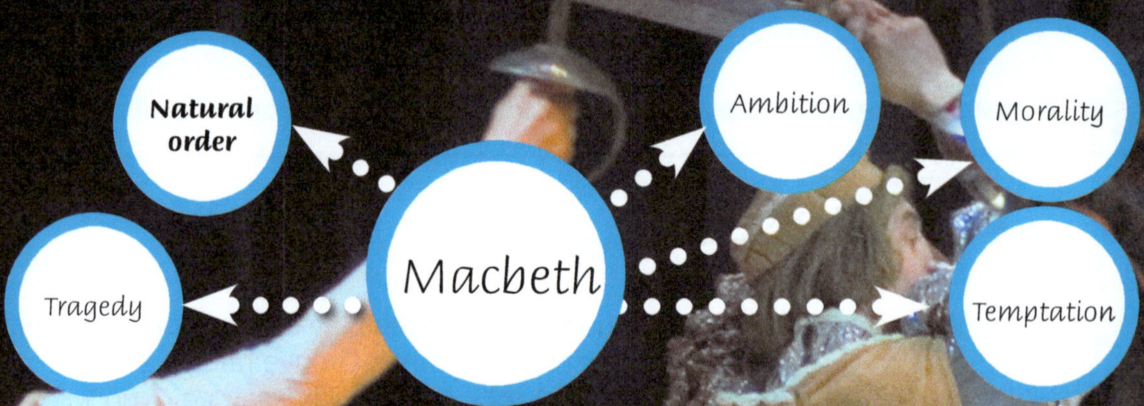

How Are the Themes Shown?

- You then need to consider how Shakespeare uses imagery, events, and characters to present each of the themes that you've identified. For example:

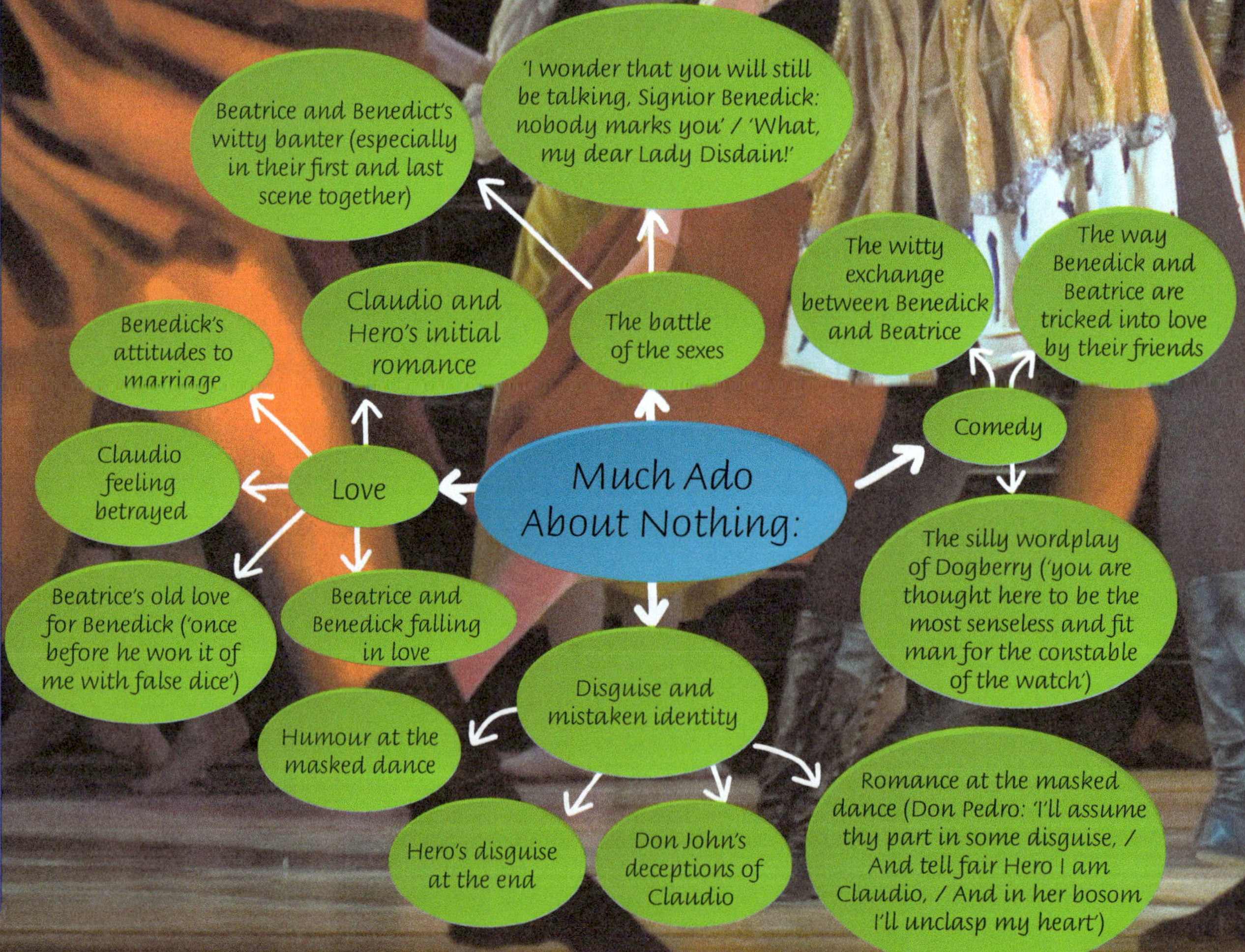

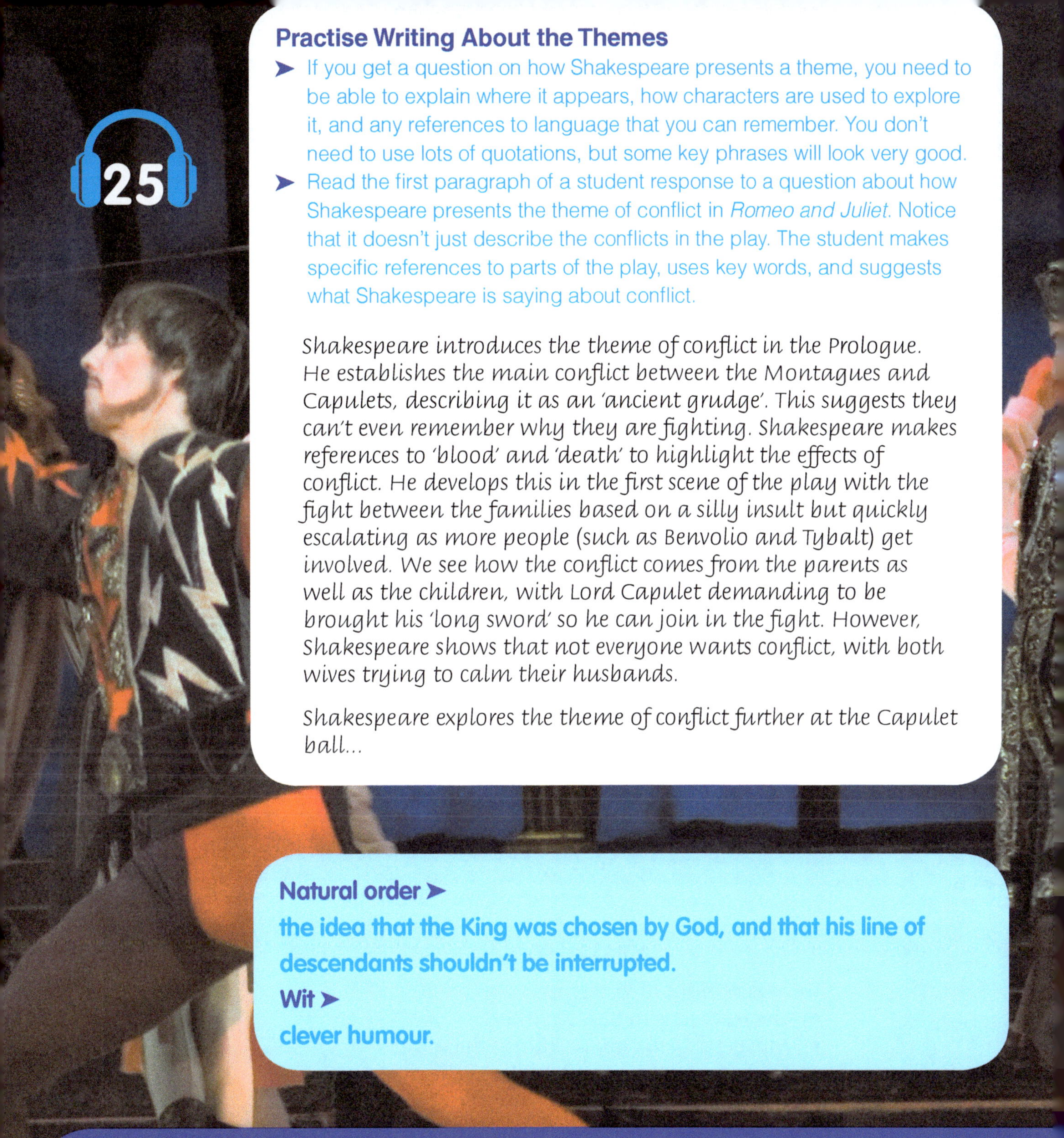

25

Practise Writing About the Themes

- If you get a question on how Shakespeare presents a theme, you need to be able to explain where it appears, how characters are used to explore it, and any references to language that you can remember. You don't need to use lots of quotations, but some key phrases will look very good.
- Read the first paragraph of a student response to a question about how Shakespeare presents the theme of conflict in *Romeo and Juliet*. Notice that it doesn't just describe the conflicts in the play. The student makes specific references to parts of the play, uses key words, and suggests what Shakespeare is saying about conflict.

Shakespeare introduces the theme of conflict in the Prologue. He establishes the main conflict between the Montagues and Capulets, describing it as an 'ancient grudge'. This suggests they can't even remember why they are fighting. Shakespeare makes references to 'blood' and 'death' to highlight the effects of conflict. He develops this in the first scene of the play with the fight between the families based on a silly insult but quickly escalating as more people (such as Benvolio and Tybalt) get involved. We see how the conflict comes from the parents as well as the children, with Lord Capulet demanding to be brought his 'long sword' so he can join in the fight. However, Shakespeare shows that not everyone wants conflict, with both wives trying to calm their husbands.

Shakespeare explores the theme of conflict further at the Capulet ball…

Natural order ➤
the idea that the King was chosen by God, and that his line of descendants shouldn't be interrupted.
Wit ➤
clever humour.

Make a theme poster for your play. Use different symbols and sketches to represent each theme and how it's shown through character and events. To develop your skills, add key quotations to help you think about Shakespeare's use of language.

1. **What are the main themes in the play you've studied?**
2. **What do you think is the most important theme in the play and why?**
3. **When writing about a theme, what areas should you focus on?**

Setting

- Setting is the time and place in which the play is set. For example:
  - *Much Ado About Nothing* — 16th century Messina (a port of Sicily)
  - *Macbeth* — 11th century Scotland
  - *Romeo and Juliet* — 14th/15th century Verona, Italy

Context

- Context refers to the historical events, attitudes, beliefs and behaviour that affect a piece of writing.
- When looking at a Shakespeare play, you should think about the context of Elizabethan/Jacobean England (when Shakespeare was writing), as well as the context of the play's setting. For example:

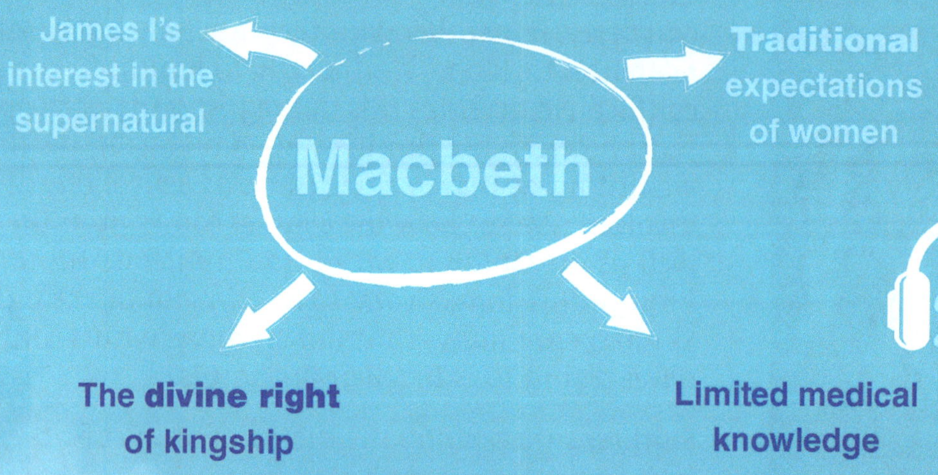

Referring To Context in Your Exam

- You need to think about how the contexts present within the play you have studied are affecting what is happening on stage. For example:

Macbeth

The divine right of kingship:

- *The references to bad weather*
- *Macbeth's fears about killing the king*
- *His feelings of guilt after killing the king and thinking he will never rest*
- *The witches and their supernatural powers*
- *The appearance of Banquo's ghost*
- *Lady Macbeth's madness*
- *The re-establishment of correct order at the end*

➤ Look at this extract from Act 2 scene 2 of *Macbeth*, after he has killed the King. How do you think the play's context shows us things about Macbeth and Lady Macbeth?

MACBETH One cried 'God bless us!' and 'Amen' the other;

As they had seen me with these hangman's hands.

Listening their fear, I could not say 'Amen,'

When they did say 'God bless us!'

LADY MACBETH Consider it not so deeply.

MACBETH But wherefore could not I pronounce 'Amen'?

I had most need of blessing, and 'Amen'

Stuck in my throat.

LADY MACBETH These deeds must not be thought

After these ways; so, it will make us mad.

MACBETH Methought I heard a voice cry 'Sleep no more!

Macbeth does murder sleep', the innocent sleep,

Sleep that knits up the ravell'd sleeve of care,

The death of each day's life, sore labour's bath,

Balm of hurt minds, great nature's second course,

Chief nourisher in life's feast,--

Macbeth's shock that he 'could not say Amen', reminds us that the play is set at a time when people were more religious. The murder of the King is a sin and this is increased for Macbeth because he would have believed in the divine right of kings, so his murder of Duncan is also an attack on God. He knows he is in need of 'blessing' because he has damned himself to Hell. The idea that he has upset the natural order of the world can be seen in his metaphorical descriptions of sleep and its 'murder'. Because of what he has done, 'great nature' will be against him and he will not get the rest and peace of mind that comes with sleep.
Lady Macbeth's response to his fears emphasise her as unwomanly for the time the play was written and set. Rather than taking his views on board and appearing submissive, she takes control and dismisses his words in short **imperative** sentences.

Divine right ➤ the idea that the king was chosen by God, and that his line of descendants should not be interrupted

Traditional ➤ a view of normality based on what has often been done in the past.

Imperative ➤ an order.

Using pictures from old magazines and the internet, make a collage that represents the setting and contexts of the play you have studied. To develop your skills, stick key quotations onto the pictures that give evidence of how the setting and context are affecting the play.

1. **What is context?**
2. **What are the setting and contexts of the play you are studying?**
3. **What does traditional mean?**

Getting Started

- When responding to an extract, you need to be more detailed and analytical because you have the text in front of you.
- Underline parts of the text that relate to the exam question and highlight specific techniques like metaphors, etc.

Analysing Character and Language

- Think about what the character is like and, considering where the extract is from in the play, whether the character has changed in any way. Then explore where you can find evidence for these characteristics in the extract.
- Look at these two short extracts of speech and the annotations done by a student.

MACBETH (ACT 3 SCENE 4)

MACBETH Then comes my fit again:
I had else been perfect;

Whole as the marble, founded as the rock,

As broad and general as the casing air:

But now, I am cabin'd, cribb'd, confin'd, bound in

To saucy doubts and fears. – But Banquo's safe?

Since killing Duncan, Macbeth has been restless/nervous.

***Pattern of three** – he wants to feel secure.*

Metaphor for paranoia.

Alliteration of harsh c sound – sound violent to emphasise his paranoia.

***Irony** in use of 'safe' (he's checking Banquo's dead) – he's lost his previous values of brotherhood, etc.*

ROMEO AND JULIET (ACT 3 SCENE 1)

LADY CAPULET Tybalt, my cousin,
O my brother's child!

O Prince, O husband, O, the blood is spill'd

Of my dear kinsman. Prince, as thou art true,

For blood of ours shed blood of Montague.

O cousin, cousin.

Repetition of 'blood' – the death has made her more aggressive.

Adjective 'dear' – she loved Tybalt as a family member.

Imperative demanding Romeo's death – she's stronger/more confident than earlier.

Repetition of 'cousin' and the exclamatory 'O' – Lady Capulet grieves over Tybalt's death. (see top line also)

Writing About Character and Language

- Write clear, concise, analytical paragraphs. A good structure to follow is:
  1. State your point about the character (you might also link this to where the extract comes from in the play).
  2. Provide a brief quotation from the extract as evidence.
  3. Analyse how the language and/or structure in your quotation shows the point that you made about character.
  4. Using a connective phrase, either develop your point with another quotation and analysis or start a new point and repeat the process.
- A paragraph of analysis using the structure above might look like this:

MUCH ADO ABOUT NOTHING (ACT 1 SCENE 3)

DON JOHN I had rather be a canker in a hedge than a rose in his grace, and it better fits my blood to be disdained of all that to fashion a carriage to rob love from any.

Don John prefers to be an outsider, 'rather be a canker in a hedge than a rose'. By having him compare himself to a wild rose, Shakespeare reminds us of his illegitimacy and the ***stigma*** *of this at the time. Similarly, Don John explains his wish to remain an outsider when he says, 'better fits my blood to be disdained of all that to fashion a carriage to rob love'. The metaphorical language shows that he refuses to change himself in order to be liked. The word 'blood' links again to his illegitimacy, suggesting he is very aware of how people view him.*

Pattern of three ➤
grouping three ideas together for emphasis.

Irony ➤
saying one thing but actually having the opposite meaning.

Stigma ➤
something that people see as a mark of disgrace.

Working with a friend, pick out three quotations for each other that show what a character is like. Write each one in the centre of a piece of A4 paper. Swap, annotate, and analyse them. Afterwards, discuss your ideas with each other.

1. How is your response to an extract expected to be different to your response to the whole text?
2. What do you need to do every time you've backed an idea up with a quotation?
3. What is irony?

Getting Started

- As with responding to an extract on character, you need to be detailed and analytical.
- Read the question carefully, then read the extract a few times and make annotations.

28

Analysing Theme and Language

- Think about how characters and events are presenting the theme, and how Shakespeare achieves this through language and structure.
- Look at this extract and a student's annotations, exploring how Shakespeare presents the theme of manipulation.

MACBETH (ACT 1 SCENE 7)

MACBETH We will proceed no further in this business:

He hath honour'd me of late; and I have bought

Golden opinions from all sorts of people,

Which would be worn now in their newest gloss,

Not cast aside so soon.

LADY MACBETH Was the hope drunk

Wherein you dress'd yourself? hath it slept since?

And wakes it now, to look so green and pale

At what it did so freely? From this time

Such I account thy love. Art thou afeard

To be the same in thine own act and valour

As thou art in desire? Wouldst thou have that

Which thou esteem'st the ornament of life,

And live a coward in thine own esteem,

Letting 'I dare not' wait upon 'I would,'

Like the poor cat i' the adage?

MACBETH Prithee, peace.

I dare do all that may become a man;

Who dares do more is none.

LADY MACBETH What beast was't, then,

That made you break this enterprise to me?

Confident statement – Macbeth is trying to take control.

Verb 'honour'd' and metaphor 'golden opinions' – Macbeth gives his reasons why he won't kill Duncan.

Pattern of three ***rhetorical questions*** *– she mocks his change of heart and calls him cowardly.*

Short sentence – claims he doesn't love her (emotional blackmail).

More rhetorical questions to make him change his mind again.

Words linked to weakness to shame him – 'afeard', 'coward', 'I dare not'.

Compares him to a small, unmanly animal.

Short sentence – Macbeth tries to take control.

Repetition of verb 'dare' – he's trying to argue back.

Use of irony to shame him – he's not a powerful beast (he's the small cat from her previous line).

When you durst do it, then you were a man;
And, to be more than what you were, you would
Be so much more the man. Nor time nor place
Did then adhere, and yet you would make both:
They have made themselves, and that their fitness now
Does unmake you. I have given suck, and know
How tender 'tis to love the babe that milks me:
I would, while it was smiling in my face,
Have pluck'd my nipple from his boneless gums,
And dash'd the brains out, had I so sworn as you
Have done to this.
MACBETH If we should fail?

Repetition of 'man' – again to make him feel unmanly. **Past tense** *to show he's being weak;* **conditional tense** *to suggest he can change.*

Verb 'unmake' – he's unmanly.

Vivid, horrific image, emphasised by verb 'dash'd' – suggesting she's stronger than Macbeth. Implies he's more like the 'babe'.

Verb 'sworn' – pointing out he's broken a promise.

The question shows Macbeth is still worried, but is again thinking about killing the king.

Writing About Theme and Language

➤ Write clear, concise, analytical paragraphs: state an idea, support it with a quotation from the text, analyse how the language or structure in your quotation shows your idea. For example:

The first way Lady Macbeth manipulates Macbeth is by suggesting he is a coward, 'Was the hope drunk / Wherein you dress'd yourself? hath it slept since? / And wakes it now, to look so green and pale / At what it did so freely?' She uses a pattern of three rhetorical questions to make Macbeth feel accused, including references to colours that symbolise cowardice (emphasised by the mocking adverb 'so') and the verb 'slept' to suggest he's passive not active.

She continues to imply his cowardice by using words that link to weakness...

Rhetorical question ➤
a question asked to make an audience think rather than answer.

Conditional tense ➤
describing things that would happen, dependent on some condition.

Past tense ➤
describing things that have happened.

Print off an extract from your play. Cut up the lines to space them out, and stick them to a piece of paper. Highlight techniques of language and structure, then add annotations about theme underneath each line.

1. **Choose a theme from your play. What scenes does this theme appear in?**
2. **When exploring how character and events show a theme, what do you need to analyse?**
3. **What is a rhetorical question?**

Shakespeare | Mind Map

Revising the Whole Text: Character, Theme, Setting and Context

- Who are your main characters?
  - What are the main characters like and do they change?
  - What key words and phrases can you remember?
  - How can you tell from things they say and do?
  - What are their key scenes?
- What are the play's main themes?
  - Which characters show each theme?
  - What events show each theme?
  - What key words and phrases can you remember?
- What are the settings and contexts of the play?
  - How does the context of the setting and of Shakespeare's time affect the play?
  - What attitudes and ideas are different in the play to today?
  - Where is the play set?

Responding to an Extract

- Read the question carefully so you know the focus.
- Read the extract several times.
- Think about where in the play the extract is from and if this affects your answer.
- Annotate relevant features of language and structure that you notice.
- Write a concise but detailed response.
- Use specific technical terms (such as verb, metaphor, etc.)
- State ideas clearly, support them with brief quotations, analyse how language and structure show your idea.

MUCH ADO ABOUT NOTHING (ACT 2 SCENE 3)

Either:

1. How far do you think Shakespeare presents Benedick as a dislikeable character?

   Write about:

   a. how Shakespeare presents Benedick in this extract

   b. how Shakespeare presents Benedick in the play as a whole.

Or:

2a. How does Shakespeare present Benedick in this extract?

2b. How is love presented elsewhere in the play?

BENEDICK I do much wonder that one man, seeing how much another man is a fool when he dedicates his behaviours to love, will, after he hath laughed at such shallow follies in others, become the argument of his own scorn by failing in love: and such a man is Claudio. I have known when there was no music with him but the drum and the fife; and now had he rather hear the tabor and the pipe: I have known when he would have walked ten mile a-foot to see a good armour; and now will he lie ten nights awake, carving the fashion of a new doublet. He was wont to speak plain and to the purpose, like an honest man and a soldier; and now is he turned orthography; his words are a very fantastical banquet, just so many strange dishes. May I be so converted and see with these eyes? I cannot tell; I think not: I will not be sworn, but love may transform me to an oyster; but I'll take my oath on it, till he have made an oyster of me, he shall never make me such a fool. One woman is fair, yet I am well; another is wise, yet I am well; another virtuous, yet I am well; but till all graces be in one woman, onc woman shall not come in my grace. Rich she shall be, that's certain; wise, or I'll none; virtuous, or I'll never cheapen her; fair, or I'll never look on her; mild, or come not near me; noble, or not I for an angel; of good discourse, an excellent musician, and her hair shall be of what colour it please God. Ha! the prince and Monsieur Love! I will hide me in the arbour.

MACBETH (ACT 1 SCENE 3)

Either:

1. How far do you think Shakespeare presents Macbeth as a good man?

   Write about:

   a. how Shakespeare presents Macbeth in this extract

   b. how Shakespeare presents Macbeth in the play as a whole.

Or:

2a. How does Shakespeare present Macbeth in this extract?

2b. How is loyalty presented elsewhere in the play?

ROSS The king hath happily received, Macbeth,
The news of thy success; and when he reads
Thy personal venture in the rebels' fight,
His wonders and his praises do contend
Which should be thine or his: silenced with that,
In viewing o'er the rest o' the selfsame day,
He finds thee in the stout Norweyan ranks,
Nothing afeard of what thyself didst make,
Strange images of death. As thick as hail
Came post with post; and every one did bear
praises in his kingdom's great defence,
And pour'd them down before him.

ANGUS We are sent
To give thee from our royal master thanks;
Only to herald thee into his sight,
Not pay thee.

ROSS And, for an earnest of a greater honour,
He bade me, from him, call thee thane of Cawdor:
In which addition, hail, most worthy thane!
For it is thine.

BANQUO What, can the devil speak true?

MACBETH The thane of Cawdor lives: why do you dress me
In borrow'd robes?

ANGUS Who was the thane lives yet;
But under heavy judgment bears that life
Which he deserves to lose. Whether he was combined
With those of Norway, or did line the rebel
With hidden help and vantage, or that with both
He labour'd in his country's wreck,
I know not;
But treasons capital, confess'd and proved,
Have overthrown him.

MACBETH (*aside*) Glamis, and thane of Cawdor!
The greatest is behind.

ROMEO AND JULIET (ACT 1 SCENE 2)

Either:

1. How far do you think Shakespeare presents Lord Capulet as a caring father?

   Write about:

   a. how Shakespeare presents Lord Capulet in this extract

   b. how Shakespeare presents Lord Capulet in the play as a whole.

Or:

2a. How does Shakespeare present Lord Capulet in this extract?

2b. How are parents presented elsewhere in the play?

CAPULET But saying o'er what I have said before:
My child is yet a stranger in the world;
She hath not seen the change of fourteen years,
Let two more summers wither in their pride,
Ere we may think her ripe to be a bride.

PARIS Younger than she are happy mothers made.

CAPULET And too soon marr'd are those so early made.
The earth hath swallow'd all my hopes but she,
She is the hopeful lady of my earth:
But woo her, gentle Paris, get her heart,
My will to her consent is but a part;
An she agree, within her scope of choice
Lies my consent and fair according voice.
This night I hold an old accustom'd feast,
Whereto I have invited many a guest,
Such as I love; and you, among the store,
One more, most welcome, makes my number more.
At my poor house look to behold this night
Earth-treading stars that make dark heaven light:
Such comfort as do lusty young men feel
When well-apparell'd April on the heel
Of limping winter treads, even such delight
Among fresh female buds shall you this night
Inherit at my house; hear all, all see,
And like her most whose merit most shall be:
Which on more view, of many mine being one
May stand in number, though in reckoning none,
Come, go with me.

Shakespeare | Exam Practice Questions

What Main Characters are Like

➤ Start by thinking about who the main characters are, what they're like at the start of the book, and how you can tell what they're like. For example:

Jane Eyre

Jane Eyre

- Unhappy childhood – orphaned; bullied by the Reeds; mistreated at Lowood by Mr Brocklehurst; about John Reed: 'every nerve I had feared him, and every morsel of flesh on my bones shrank when he came near'.
- Determined – stands up to Mrs Reed; tries to better herself at Lowood; wants to be free and independent; 'a fondness for some of my studies, and a desire to excel in all'.
- Caring – stays with Helen on her deathbed; cares for Adele; helps Rochester when he falls from his horse; 'I'll stay with you, dear Helen: no one shall take me away'.

Edward Rochester

- Rude – he is initially rude to Jane; he is off-hand with Mrs Fairfax; he won't pretend to be nice in polite company; 'he would sometimes pass me haughtily or coldly'.
- Passionate – he follows his heart rather than social conventions; 'I have a right to get pleasure out of life: and I will get it, cost what it may'.
- Mysterious – we don't realise who he is at first; strange events in the house, such as the fire in his room; his strange relationship with Richard Mason; 'Mrs Fairfax either could not, or would not, give me more explicit information of the origin and nature of Mr Rochester's trials'.

➤ You need to revise which events in the novel are important for showing what your characters are like. It's a bonus if you can also learn some key quotations allowing you to analyse the writer's use of language.

Context ➤
the historical events, attitudes, beliefs and behaviour that affect a piece of writing (due to when it was written and/or set).

Characters and Context

➤ It's important to think about how the characters are affected by the **context** of the novel. This can help us to understand their behaviour or how others react to them. For example:

The Strange Case of Dr Jekyll and Mr Hyde – Dr Henry Jekyll

Victorian Values	How These Affect His Characterisation
Christianity	Jekyll sees Hyde as the battle between good and evil within him: 'the spirit of hell awoke in me and raged'. Hyde commits immoral crimes that shock Jekyll.
Proper social conduct	Jekyll, as a respected gentleman, cannot behave how he wants to; his experiments lead him to create Mr Hyde (allowing him to hide his improper conduct and 'pleasures').
Intolerance of crime	Shocked at the murder of Carew, Jekyll tries to resist becoming Hyde: 'I embraced anew the restrictions of natural life'.

How Main Characters Change

➤ Once you've established what your main characters are like, you need to explore how they change or develop. Think about how you can tell this from how the characters speak and behave during key scenes in the book. For example:

Great Expectations

- Unhappy childhood but loves Joe.
- Desperate for Estella to love him.

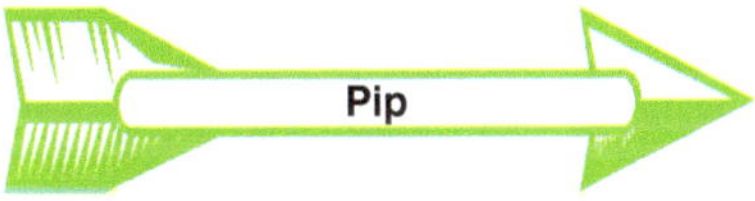

- Becomes a gentleman.
- Is ashamed of Joe.
- Increasingly selfish.
- Develops a conscience, is remorseful and works hard to make up for his mistakes.

29

Make your own character magazine. For each character, include: a sketch; fact-file; a timeline of what the character is like, how they change, and why; key quotes of description and speech. To develop your skills, choose a characteristic of each character and include a paragraph analysing how it's shown.

1. **Who are the main characters in your novel?**
2. **What are these characters like and how do they change or develop?**
3. **How are they affected by the novel's context?**

Identify Settings

- Start by identifying the main settings in your novel. Try to also identify some key quotations about each setting. For example:

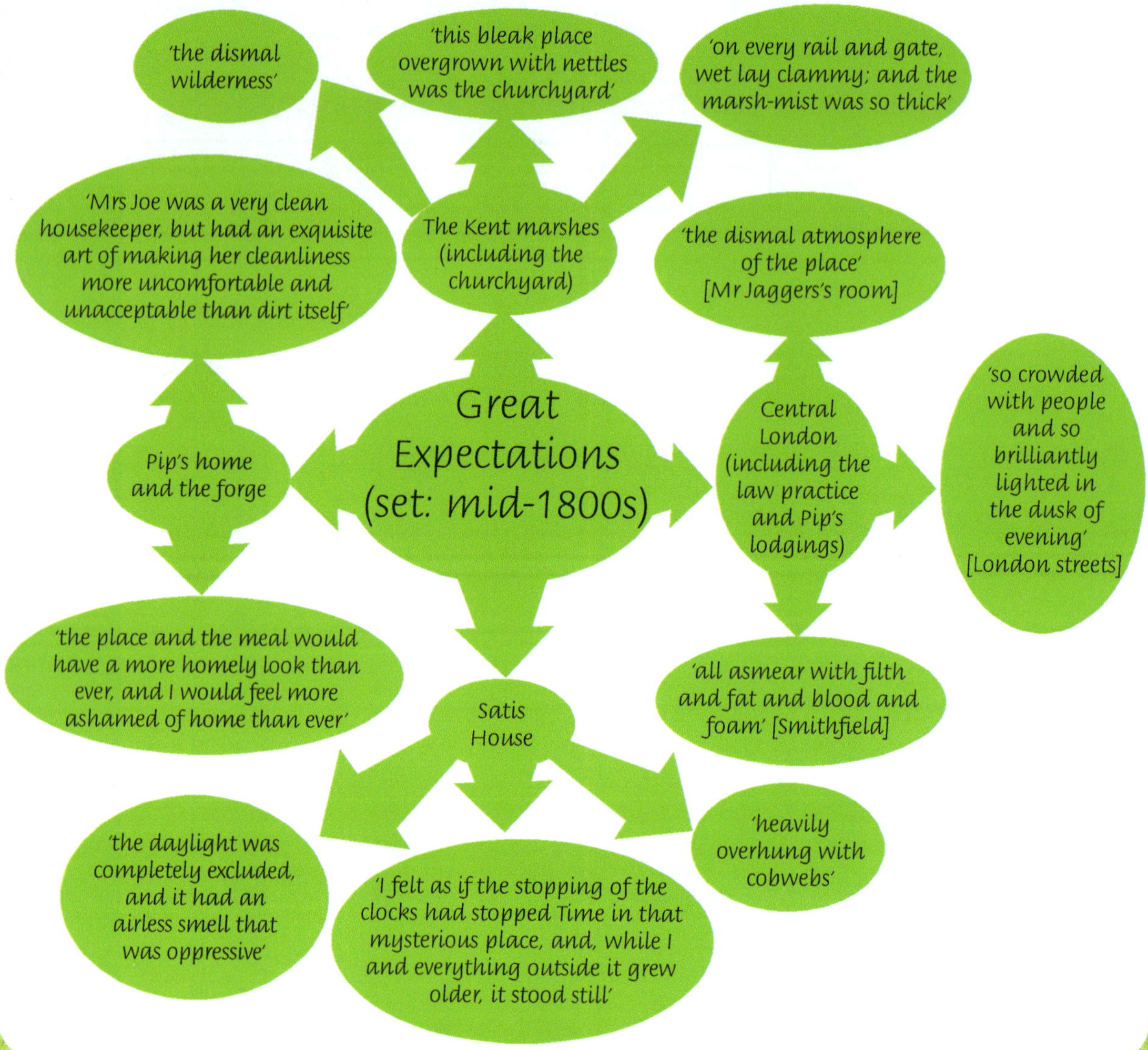

How Settings are Presented

- Practise analysing how the author uses different features of language and structure to convey what different settings are like (their appearance and **atmosphere**). For example:

*Charlotte Bronte presents Thornfield as unwelcoming, 'A very chill and vault-like air pervaded the stairs and gallery, suggesting cheerless ideas of space and solitude'. Images of coldness are emphasised by the simile that links the house to a tomb, and by the verb 'pervaded' which suggests this unpleasant atmosphere is everywhere. This coldness is **literal** but also links to emotional coldness through the adjective 'cheerless' which makes it clear that the 'solitude' is lonely rather than peaceful.*

Clear point about setting

Evidence containing interesting language

Analysis of how specific words and phrases link to the point being made about the setting

30

Atmosphere ➤
the emotion or feeling of a piece of writing.

Literal ➤
the basic, surface meaning.

What Settings Add to the Novel

➤ As well as being aware of how the settings are presented by the author, you should also revise how the settings help you understand things about the characters, themes, and context of the novel. For example:

The contrasts between the descriptions of the Kent marshes and central London in Great Expectations help us to explore the theme of class in the mid 1800s.

The descriptions of Thornfield in Jane Eyre show us aspects of Rochester's character.

In The Strange Case of Dr Jekyll and Mr Hyde, comparing the front and side entrance of Dr Jekyll's house links to the respectable, socially-acceptable facade that he puts on in life.

Create posters for each of your settings, either by drawing them or using images from magazines and the internet. Accompany your images with key quotations from the novel about each setting. To develop your skills, add extra labels (using two different colours) about how the settings link to character or theme.

1. **What are the main settings in your novel?**
2. **How do the settings help to tell you about character?**
3. **How do the settings link to theme?**

31

Identify Main Themes

- Start by identifying the main ideas that the writer is exploring in their novel. For example, in Great Expectations:

Family

Class and Ambition

Guilt

Love

Crime

Growing up

How Themes are Presented

- Decide which characters and events in your novel help to introduce or develop each of your themes. Find key quotations from the novel that show how the theme is expressed and consider whether the theme is being affected by the novel's context. For example:

Dr Jekyll and Mr Hyde: Reputation

- Jekyll's wish to keep up his **reputation** leads to the creation of Hyde
  - ('I concealed my pleasures')
  - Link to Victorian values about class and respectability
- Jekyll's fear that the Carew murder case might ruin his reputation
  - ('I was thinking of my own character, which this hateful business has rather exposed')
  - Increase in newspaper readership meant that issues such as crimes and court cases could be more widely reported.
- Utterson and Enfield believe in avoiding gossip
  - Link to ideas of proper social conduct.
  - ('I feel very strongly about putting questions; it partakes too much of the style of the day of judgement')
- Utterson covering up for Dr Jekyll
  - ('I would say nothing of this paper. If your master has fled or is dead, we may at least save his credit')
  - Link to the importance of respectability and status.

How to Write About Themes

➤ Writing about themes is the same as writing about character or setting. Make clear points, support them with quotations as evidence, and analyse how the author's use of language or structure gets across the point you have made.

One way in which the theme of social class is presented in Jane Eyre is through the way Jane thinks that she is not good enough for Rochester, 'I know I must conceal my sentiments: I must smother hope; I must remember that he cannot care much for me'. The use of the metaphor about smothering hope reminds us that love between the social classes was rare in Victorian England. This is emphasised by the verbs 'know' and 'remember' that imply people had a clear social position that they were aware of and should not try to move beyond. The use of the negative verb 'cannot' indicates that ***social expectations*** *trap all classes as, here, they affect Rochester not Jane. The pattern of three, using the imperative verb 'must', suggests that Jane also fears for her job should the truth come out, which links to the vulnerability of women and the lower classes.*

- Clear point about the theme
- Evidence
- Analysis of specific features of language or structure
- Links to context
- Further analysis if possible; not just moving on to the next point

Ambition ➤
desire to succeed in some way.

Reputation ➤
the opinions that people have formed about someone.

Social expectations ➤
how society expects people to behave.

On a sheet of A3 paper, create theme pyramids. You are only allowed one word for the top layer: this should be your theme, such as 'Love'. For the second layer, you are allowed two single words or a two-word phrase; for the third layer, you are allowed three words, etc. Using ten layers for each of your pyramids, try to summarise the main points about each theme in your novel.

1. What are the main themes in your novel?
2. How do they link to characters and events?
3. How do the novel's themes link to its context?

19th Century Fiction | Mind Map

19th Century Fiction

State an idea, support it with evidence, analyse how features of language or structure have conveyed your idea.

Who are your main characters and how do they develop?

What are the main settings of the novel? What can they tell you about characters?

What are the main themes of your novel? How are they shown through character, setting and events?

What are the contexts within your novel? How do they affect character and events?

What key quotations can you find about character, setting and theme?

1. *The Strange Case of Dr Jekyll and Mr Hyde*

How does Stevenson create an atmosphere of horror through the characters of Dr Jekyll and Mr Hyde?

2. *Great Expectations*

Using this extract as a starting point, how does Dickens present Miss Havisham as a disturbing character?

> I saw that the bride within the bridal dress had withered like the dress, and like the flowers, and had no brightness left but the brightness of her sunken eyes. I saw that the dress had been put upon the rounded figure of a young woman, and that the figure upon which it now hung loose had shrunk to skin and bone. Once, I had been taken to see some ghastly waxwork at the Fair, representing I know not what impossible personage lying in state. Once, I had been taken to one of our old marsh churches to see a skeleton in the ashes of a rich dress that had been dug out of a vault under the church pavement. Now, waxwork and skeleton seemed to have dark eyes that moved and looked at me. I should have cried out, if I could.
>
> "Who is it?" said the lady at the table.
>
> "Pip, ma'am."
>
> "Pip?"
>
> "Mr. Pumblechook's boy, ma'am. Come—to play."
>
> "Come nearer; let me look at you. Come close."
>
> It was when I stood before her, avoiding her eyes, that I took note of the surrounding objects in detail, and saw that her watch had stopped at twenty minutes to nine, and that a clock in the room had stopped at twenty minutes to nine.
>
> "Look at me," said Miss Havisham. "You are not afraid of a woman who has never seen the sun since you were born?"
>
> I regret to state that I was not afraid of telling the enormous lie comprehended in the answer "No."
>
> "Do you know what I touch here?" she said, laying her hands, one upon the other, on her left side.
>
> "Yes, ma'am." (It made me think of the young man.)
>
> "What do I touch?"
>
> "Your heart."
>
> "Broken!"
>
> She uttered the word with an eager look, and with strong emphasis, and with a weird smile that had a kind of boast in it. Afterwards she kept her hands there for a little while, and slowly took them away as if they were heavy.

3. *Jane Eyre*

How is the theme of cruelty presented at two different points in the novel?

> To generate your own questions, choose a character or theme in the novel and ask yourself how it has been presented. Either write about two different points in the novel, or give yourself a short extract as a starting point and then write about the novel as a whole.

Module 1 | Revising Character

The Main Characters

➤ Start by identifying your main characters and their characteristics at the start of the story. Think about:

Physical ➤ to do with the body.
Connectives ➤ joining words or phrases.
Consequence ➤ the effect or result of something.

Character

- their relationships
- what others say about them
- their actions
- how the writer uses language to portray them
- what they say and how they say it

➤ Make sure you can evidence your ideas about character, either through key quotations or referring to specific events in the text. For example:

Piggy from *Lord of the Flies*

- Lots of **physical** descriptions: 'the fat boy', 'he wiped his glasses and adjusted them on his button nose'; 'Piggy flushed suddenly'.
- He's shy with people ('waited to be asked his name'); he likes Ralph, who grows to like him back; he's bullied by people like Jack ('Shut up, Fatty').
- He complains and sounds weak ('I can't swim. I wasn't allowed. My asthma –'); he's sensible and makes plans ('We can use this to call the others. Have a meeting.'); he's not as educated as the others ('All them other kids').
- He tries to organise people (such as getting people's names at the start); he looks after the younger children ('Let him have the conch!') but gets annoyed when people are immature ('Like a crowd of kids').
- Jack is rude to Piggy as he sees him as inferior; Ralph begins to stand up for him ('Piggy's got the conch').

32

Character Development

- You should consider whether your characters change during the story. Do the five character areas opposite remain constant or not? For example:

Sheila Birling in *An Inspector Calls*	
The start of Act 1...	**As the play develops...**
Self-centred and uncaring	Guilty and more thoughtful
Close to her mum and dad	Rebels a little against her parents
Critical of others but defensive of herself	More responsible for her actions
Excitable	More mature
Quite naive	Wiser (about how her actions affect others)

- Practise writing paragraphs about how characters change, making use of **connectives** of comparison, time, and **consequence**. Look at this example of a student's revision work about how Sheila changes:

At the start of the play, Sheila is very defensive, 'What do you mean by saying that? You talk as if we were responsible –'. Her rhetorical question, aimed at the Inspector, has an accusatory tone which suggests she doesn't expect to be spoken to in this manner. The use of the phrase 'as if' shows she doesn't consider her family responsible for Eva's death.

Connective of time and a clear point

Evidence

Analysis of language features

As a result of the Inspector's questioning, she begins to accept the consequences of her actions in Act 2: 'And I know I'm to blame – and I'm desperately sorry – but I can't believe – I won't believe – it's simply my fault'. The use of dashes to create pauses in her speech shows how upset she is. This is emphasised by her acceptance of 'blame' and the adverb 'desperately'. However, the repeating negatives ('can't... won't') indicate she's still in a state of denial.

Connective of consequence and a clear point

Evidence

Analysis of sentence structure

Connective of comparison

Make a paper chain of men and women to represent the characters in your story, and label them with lots of information. Try to include the different things mentioned in the 'Main Characters' section. To develop your skills, include labels about how each character develops on the backs of the paper chain figures.

1. **Who are your main characters?**
2. **What five words would you use to describe each of your main characters?**
3. **How do your main characters change?**

Module 2 | Revising Themes

Identifying Your Themes

- Start by deciding what the main ideas are in the text you are studying. For example:

DNA

- **Morality**
- Crime and guilt
- Gangs and peer pressure

Lord of the Flies

- Fear
- Leadership and power
- Human nature

An Inspector Calls

- Morality
- **Class**
- Truth and justice

Exploring Your Themes

- Think about how your text's themes are shown through character and plot, noting down key quotations. For example:

Lord of the Flies: Leadership and Power

- Jack and Ralph struggle for power. Disagreement and difference throughout, especially about fire and shelters vs hunting. ('The two boys faced each other. There was the brilliant world of hunting, tactics, fierce exhilaration, skill; and there was the world of longing and baffled common-sense.')
- Jack sees leadership as aggression. Jack's treatment of the choir and his rule of Castle Rock. ('We'll have rules!' he cried excitedly. 'Lots of rules! Then when anyone breaks 'em – ')
- Ralph sees leadership as discussion. Early chapters where Ralph calls meetings. ('I'm calling an assembly')
- The conch is a symbol of **democracy**. Piggy and Ralph value the conch; it's broken when Piggy is killed. ('I got the conch,' said Piggy, in a hurt voice. 'I got a right to speak.')
- The children need a leader. They come when called at the start and always need rules. ('The children gave him the same simple obedience that they had given to the men with the megaphones.')

33

Analysing Language and Structure

➤ You need to be able to write about how themes are shown through the writer's use of language and structure. Using the themes you've identified (your points) and the key quotations you've found (your evidence), practise analysing how themes are presented. For example:

DNA

One way in which Dennis Kelly presents the theme of control is through John Tate and his banning of the word dead, 'New rule; that word is banned and if anyone says it I'm going to have to, you know, bite their face. Or something.' The pause created by the semi-colon after the word 'rule' and the use of the adjective 'banned' show John Tate takes charge of the gang. He maintains his control through specific threats of violence, with the verb 'bite', and more frightening, unspecific threats: the short sentence makes the vagueness of 'Or something' stand out, so the characters and the audience have to imagine what John could do.

- Clear point about theme, linked to character and event
- Well-chosen quotation with plenty to analyse
- Analysis of sentence structure
- Analysis of language, using technical terms
- Development of analysis

Morality ➤
seeing the difference between good and bad.

Class ➤
social groupings (i.e. upper, middle, lower) based on wealth, education, etc.

Democracy ➤
a form of government controlled by the people that offers equality through voting and elections.

Find a series of objects or pictures to represent the different themes in your text. Write key quotes on small cards to show the characters and events that link to each theme, and tie them to your pictures and objects. To develop your skills, write point, evidence, analysis (PEA) paragraphs on the back of each card, using different colours for your point, your evidence, and your analysis.

1. **What are the key themes in your text?**
2. **Which characters and events link to each of your themes?**
3. **In your text, which themes create conflict between characters?**

Play or Novel?

- You need to think about whether your 20th century fiction text is a play or novel, and how this affects the ways in which meaning is conveyed to the audience.
- Novelists include detailed descriptions of setting so the reader can fully imagine where the story takes place. However, a play is written to be performed with **dialogue**, so a playwright will use **stage directions** to establish important items (such as furniture) and their location on stage, and how music and lighting should be used to add atmosphere.

34

Settings

- A novel will usually have a wider variety of settings to a play (because they can be easily described, whereas a play would need to keep changing the set); however, a play will sometimes make much more specific use of time in order to make it clear how a story is unfolding on stage.
- Start by identifying your different settings, where in the text they are used, and key quotations. For example:

Animal Farm

Setting	Chapters	Key Quotations (and notes on features of language and structure)
The fields	Chapters 2, 3, 5, 7	'The grass and the bursting hedges were gilded by the level rays of the sun' (metaphor)
The farmhouse	Chapters 2, 6	'gazing with a kind of awe at the unbelievable luxury' (verb, nouns and adjective)

Dialogue ➤
speech between two or more characters.

Stage direction ➤
information on how a play should look and be performed.

Symbolise ➤
when an object or image represents some other meaning.

Writing About Setting

- When exploring setting, think about what it's like, how this has been achieved by the writer, and how it relates to the context. You should also think about how a setting helps us to understand things about character or theme. Look at these revision notes by a student about the opening stage directions from *An Inspector Calls*:

Dining room of a fairly large suburban house, belonging to a fairly prosperous manufacturer. It is a solidly built room, with good solid furniture of the period. A little upstage of centre is a solid but not too large dining room table with a solid set of dining room chairs around it. A few imposing but tasteless pictures and engravings. The general effect is substantial and comfortable and old-fashioned but not cosy and homelike.

The size of the room ('fairly large') indicates the family's wealth and links to the theme of class.

The repeated use of 'solid' furniture **symbolises** *the family's confidence and again links to class.*

The furniture is 'period' so the audience can recognise the setting as early 20th century.

The dining room setting links to theme of family and shows they are close but also quite formal. The fact it isn't 'cosy' might suggest a lack of love.

The room and its furnishings should show elements of Mr Birling's character (as he is the head of the house). The paintings ('imposing but tasteless') symbolise his desire to show off his wealth, but his lack of sensitivity; he values money over all things.

The room should seem 'comfortable' so when the Inspector arrives he stands out more and seems to clash with the setting.

Important Contexts

- Think about the different things that might affect the way in which the story was written and the way in which we receive it. This might include when the story was written, when it is set, the social groupings of the characters, what sort of person the story was written by, etc. For example:

Lord of the Flies: Context

- William Golding was a schoolteacher
- The novel was published in 1954, soon after the horrors of WW2
- The setting is a desert island with no adults
- British politics was dominated by ex-public schoolboys
- The book presents boys of different class and attitude

Think about your settings by drawing them, building a mini stage set, or turning them into a map.

1. **What are the settings and contexts of your text?**
2. **How do they tell you things about the story's characters?**
3. **How do they tell you things about the story's themes?**

Modern Fiction | Mind Map

Modern Fiction

- Who are your main characters and how do they develop?
- What are the main settings of the text? What can they tell you about characters?
- What are the main themes of your text? How are they shown through character, setting and events?
- Have you studied a novel or a play? How does this affect the ways in which character, theme and setting are presented?
- What key quotations can you find about character, setting and theme?
- State an idea, support it with evidence, analyse how features of language or structure have conveyed your idea.

1. *DNA*

'They might even give me money for it, do you think I should ask for money?' How does Dennis Kelly develop the character of Cathy?

2. *Lord of the Flies*

Choose one point in the novel where conflict is shown and explain how it is presented by the author.

3. *Animal Farm*

'Though not yet full-grown they were huge dogs, and as fierce-looking as wolves. They kept close to Napoleon. It was noticed that they wagged their tails to him in the same way as the other dogs had been used to do to Mr Jones.'

How does George Orwell present the theme of power? Refer to the context of the novel.

4. *An Inspector Calls*

'But you're partly to blame. Just as your father is.'

How does J B Priestley present the character of Inspector Goole?

To generate your own questions, choose a character or theme in the text. Ask yourself how it has been presented through the author's use of language, structure and form.

Answers

Unseen Non-Fiction

pages 4–5

1. Purpose, audience, form.
2. Inform, explain, describe, argue, persuade, instruct, advise, review.
3. Adults, teenagers, your headteacher, governors, MPs/councillors, pensioners, locals, etc.
4. Newspapers, magazines, encyclopaedia entries, adverts, web-pages, letters, reviews, autobiographies, biographies, etc.

pages 6–7

1. Something that can be proven.
2. Something that people think or feel.
3. At the start of paragraphs.
4. To show you fully understand the text.

pages 8–9

1. Verb = a word that describes an action; noun = thing/object word; adjective = a word that describes a noun;
   adverb = a word that describes a verb.
2. Short sentences, lists, exclamations, questions, use of colons, etc.
3. Start, middle, end.

pages 10–11

1. So you know, specifically, what to compare.
2. A point of comparison, a quotation, explanation/analysis.
3. Similarly, however, whereas, on the other hand, in comparison, in contrast, just as, etc.

pages 12–13

1. Longer sentences, more formal writing, old-fashioned or more complex vocabulary.
2. Points, evidence, analysis.
3. Diary and autobiography. Similar = written by the person they're about, so personal, will contain lots of opinions. Difference = diary written at the time, autobiography written later; diary more personal and, unlike an autobiography, not written to be read so may be more honest and contain 'secrets'; autobiography may be more entertaining and descriptive as it's written to be sold.

page 15 Practice Questions

1. One mark each for any two of the following: St Wilfrid's is in Hulme; it opened in 1842; its walls are white-washed; there are cloakrooms; the headmaster is Mr Coleman; there is a nun called Mother Peter; the youngest teacher is Mr Callaghan.
2. One mark for each of the following: apprehension (or fear); unhappiness (or upset).
3. One mark for any two of the following, plus a mark for a clear explanation of how the quotation shows unhappiness: 'soaked by rain'; 'dumped, as we are'; 'no money to be had and there are no resources'; 'no colour and no laughter'; 'slackly shaped and contaminated... stink'; 'will faint due to lack of food'.
4. 5–6 marks (Level 7–9) for a detailed response, using several well-chosen quotations, and offering specific explanations and inferences about what Mr Coleman is like.
   3–4 marks (Level 4–6) for a clear understanding, with two quotations and generally clear explanations.
   1–2 marks (Level 1–3) for showing some awareness of what Mr Coleman is like, supported by a quotation or a reference to the text.
5. 10–12 marks (Level 8–9) for a detailed response that shows a perceptive response to language and structure, selecting a range of good quotations, and using terminology to analyse a variety of effects achieved by the writer.
   7–9 marks (Level 6–7) for a clear response, supported by several, relevant quotations, with some technical analysis of different language and structure effects achieved.
   4–6 marks (Level 4–5) for some understanding of language and structure, supported by some relevant quotations, and some explanation of different techniques used.
   1–3 marks (Level 1–3) for a simple answer that displays some awareness of language, with some references to the text and clear descriptions of what they show.

Unseen Fiction

pages 16–17

1. So you know, specifically, what type of information you need and where you should retrieve it from.
2. Capital letters to help you spot names of people, places, etc., and numbers to help you spot dates, ages, statistics, etc.
3. Synonyms can help you find sections of the text that relate to the theme you've been given.

pages 18–19

1. Sentence structure = the way punctuation and sentence types have been used to convey information in different ways. Narrative structure = how the whole text has been organised in order to establish and develop ideas.
2. Short sentences, long sentences, lists, dashes, ellipses, exclamations, questions, etc.
3. Start, middle, end.

pages 20–21

1. Character, setting, mood.
2. *What* helps you to establish the idea that has been conveyed, whilst *How* pushes you to analyse the different features of language that have been used to achieve this.
3. Verbs, adjectives, adverbs, simile, metaphor, personifications, images, contrasts, etc.

pages 22–23

1. Connectives of comparison. For example: Similarly, Whereas, Just as.
2. You need to come up with ideas. Make a Venn diagram or mind map.
3. Language and structure.

page 25 Practice Questions

1. One mark each for any four of the following: Miranda goes to boarding school; she lives opposite the Town Hall Annexe; she has a younger sister; she uses the library; she has blonde hair / wears her hair in a pigtail.
2. Level 8–9: a detailed understanding of how the opening is structured and its effect on the reader, for example holding back and building up details about Miranda (from her appearance to her actual name), making the narrator seem increasingly strange and obsessive, and indicating that he will get to know her; well-chosen quotations and perceptive explanations that make good use of inference.
   Level 4–5: clear references to the start, middle and end of the passage, focussing on what we find out about Miranda and some comments about the reader's response to the narrator; several, relevant, well-explained quotations with some inference.
3. Level 8–9: a detailed response to language, with well-chosen quotations that show or suggest the narrator's obsession with Miranda; a range of terminology used to analyse how meaning is conveyed to the reader.
   Level 4–5: a clear understanding of how language is used to make the narrator seem obsessive; several, relevant quotations, with clear explanations and some comments on the effects of specific techniques.
4. Level 8–9: a balanced response, but with clear judgements, analysing how the narrator is presented as romantic and how he is presented as frightening; well-chosen quotations and a range of technical analysis of how meaning is conveyed.
   Level 4–5: a clear response and judgement, but tending to focus more on one side of the argument; several, relevant quotations, with clear explanations and some comments on the effects of specific techniques.
5. Level 8–9: a well-structured comparison, offering a perceptive understanding of character; well-chosen quotations and detailed analysis of how language and structure are used to convey meaning, make use of a range of terminology.
   Level 4–5: a clear understanding of the two characters, with several points of comparison; relevant quotations are used to support most ideas, with clear explanations of how they reveal character and some comments on the effects of specific techniques.

Writing

pages 26–27

1. Facts and statistics.
2. Connectives of time and place.
3. Thematically or chronologically.

pages 28–29

1. Cause and effect.
2. Connectives of cause/effect and comparison.
3. Present tense if a current issue; past tense if about something that's already happened.

pages 30–31

1. A series of vivid pictures in their head.
2. Adjective, adverbs, simile, metaphor, personification, images, contrasts, senses, onomatopoeia, alliteration, sibilance, etc.
3. Short sentence to surprise; compound sentences to create contrasts; complex sentences to include lots of detail; lists to build up ideas.

pages 32–33

1. The audience's opinions.
2. FORESTRY.
3. Facts, Opinions, Rhetorical questions, Empathy and emotive language, Statistics, Triplets, Repetition, You.

pages 34–35

1. You're presenting both sides of the argument, not just your opinion.
2. A conclusion or summary that gives your final judgement.
3. Connectives of comparison, contrast, and cause/effect.

pages 36–37

1. So the audience can understand the different stages you want them to follow.
2. Modal verbs suggest necessity or choice; they allow you to insist on, or suggest, different things for the audience to do.
3. A friendly tone is needed to make the audience feel that you understand them or are on their side.

pages 38–39

1. For example: ambition, correction, fiction, imagination, nation, operation, pollution, situation, translation, etc.
2. There points out a place; their indicates ownership; they're is an abbreviation of they are.
3. For example: weight (how heavy something is) + wait (to pause).

pages 40–41

1. Simple, compound, complex.
2. To show the start of a sentence or to indicate a proper noun (name of a person, place or establishment).
3. To indicate abbreviation or ownership.

pages 44–45 Practice Questions

Q1–7.

Marks allocated for how successfully the piece of writing meets the requirements of the task, and for accuracy of spelling, punctuation and grammar.

Level 8–9: convincing and engaging writing throughout; writing fully matched to required purpose, audience and form; sustained use of ambitious vocabulary and a range of techniques; well-structured and fully developed, with complex ideas; varied and inventive structural features, with fluently linked paragraphs; a wide range of punctuation and the full range of sentence structures are used accurately and consistently; complex grammar and spelling are secure.

Level 4–5: clear writing throughout; writing is generally matched to required purpose, audience and form; vocabulary and some techniques chosen successfully for effect; ideas are clearly connected and paragraphs are mostly appropriate with some structural features to keep meaning clear; punctuation and sentences are generally accurate, with some range of structures used for effect; grammar is mostly secure and spelling of familiar, complex words is accurate.

Poetry

pages 46–47

1. Verb = doing word; adjective = a word that describes a noun; adverb = a word that describes a verb.

2. Simile = a comparison using 'like' or 'as'; metaphor = a comparison that's impossible but is written as if it's true.
3. Short sentences, lists, pattern of three, repetition, exclamation, enjambment, etc.

pages 48–49

1. Themes, Imagery, Form, Structure.
2. How it's conveying the theme.
3. Form = the type of poem and its shape (including number of stanzas, rhyme, line-length, etc).

pages 50–51

1. Themes, imagery, form, structure.
2. Make a clear point, support it with a quotation as evidence, and analyse how the language, form or structure within your quotation gets across the point you made.
3. A traditional form of love poetry, containing 14 lines, 10 syllables per line, and a clear rhyme scheme.

pages 52–53

1. Themes, imagery, form, structure.
2. Connectives of comparison.
3. An everyday or slang word/phrase.

pages 54–55

1. The language may be more familiar/easy.
2. Connectives of comparison.
3. Repetition of s sounds at the start of, or within, words.

page 57 Practice Questions

Q1 and **Q3.**

Level 8–9: a detailed, perceptive and focussed comparison, with a variety of links providing a full exploration of ideas, viewpoints and contexts; well-chosen, precise references; a range of terminology used to analyse the different methods of language, structure and form by which the poets convey meaning.

Level 4–5: a clear, mostly sustained comparison, focussed on the question, with specific links showing a good understanding of ideas, viewpoints and contexts; relevant references and clear explanations of several different ways in which poets use language, structure and form to convey meaning; some use of terminology.

Q2.

Level 8–9: a detailed, perceptive and focussed response, presenting a variety of ideas; well-chosen, precise quotations; a range of terminology used to analyse the different methods of language, structure and form by which the poet conveys meaning.

Level 4–5: a clear response, mostly focussed on the question, with a number of ideas showing a good understanding of the poem; relevant quotations and clear explanations of different ways in which the poet uses language, structure and form to convey meaning; some use of terminology.

Q2 Possible Content:

- Short sentence at the start to emphasise shock.
- Use of adjectives 'small feverish' to show concern.
- Use of verb 'knelt' to suggest begging/desperation.
- Repetition of 'shook you' to show terror.
- Contrasting the nice 'blue' of the blanket to the way the 'blue' of the face implies death.
- Rhetorical question to show shock at what she might have to do.
- Simile to show her panic.
- Repetition of intensifier 'so' to show her desperation.
- 'Oh Jesus' suggests surprise and relief, as well as a prayer of thanks.
- Repetition of 'you' and 'your' throughout shows the importance of the child.

Q3 Possible Content:

- Clear love for the children.
- Both children seem beautiful and tiny.
- Both poets fear for their children's lives.
- One mother seems quite confident in what to do, the other seems unsure.
- Feeling happy and impressed that both children are strong.

Shakespeare

pages 58–59

1. What they're like and how their character develops.
2. For example: Lady Macbeth – ambitious, controlling, scheming, domineering.
3. For example: unable to control Macbeth's behaviour; mad and unable to rest; full of guilt for what she has done.

pages 60–61

1. For example: *Romeo and Juliet* – love, tragedy, time, fate, family, conflict.
2. For example: *Macbeth* – ambition because it's the driving force for the things that Macbeth and Lady Macbeth do, as well as the way in which the witches trick Macbeth.
3. Where the theme appears, how characters are used to explore it, and how their language links to the theme.

pages 62–63

1. Context = the historical events, attitudes, beliefs and behaviour that affect a piece of writing.
2. For example: *Much Ado About Nothing* – courtly behaviour, traditional expectations of women, attitudes towards illegitimacy and sex before marriage.
3. Traditional = a view of normality based on what has happened in the past.

pages 64–65

1. You need to be more detailed and analytical because you have the text in front of you.
2. Analyse how different features of language and structure in your quotation convey meaning.

3. Saying one thing but actually having the opposite meaning.

pages 66–67

1. For example: the theme of parents and children in *Romeo and Juliet* – Act 1 scene 2 and 3, Act 3 scene 5, Act 4 scene 5, Act 5 scene 3.
2. How features of language, structure and form show the theme.
3. A question asked to make the audience think rather than answer.

pages 69–71: Practice Questions

Part a. (response to an extract).

Level 8–9: a detailed, focussed and cohesive response; well-chosen, subtle quotations; sustained, perceptive analysis of language, structure and form, making use of a range of terminology to explore the effects on the audience.
Level 4–5: a clear, mostly focussed response; a variety of relevant quotations; clear explanations of how language, structure and form convey meaning, with some terminology, showing a good understanding of the effects on the audience.

Part b. (response to the whole text).

Level 8–9: a personal, focussed and well-developed response; a wide range of points supported by well-chosen references; detailed understanding of the effects of context on the play.
Level 4–5: a relevant, focussed response with some development; some range of points supported by relevant references; clear comments on the effects of context on the play.

Page 69: Possible Content

- Benedick scorns love and people who fall in love.
- He is scornful of Claudio falling love after saying he wouldn't (which is ironic as Benedick later does the same).
- Benedick sees things to do with being a soldier as manly, and things to do with love as unmanly and foolish.
- Benedick wonders whether he too could fall in love, but decides he won't.
- He doesn't believe his ideal woman exists; he expects a woman to be perfect.
- He makes jokes, such as listing the qualities a woman must have and then saying that he doesn't mind about her hair colour.
- Benedick is quite mischievous: mocking his friends and then hiding from them.

Elsewhere in the play, Benedick is presented as mostly popular and funny. He is rude (when talking to Beatrice) and likes to be the centre of attention. However, he is more honest about his feelings for her when he finds she loves him back. He shows honour in his willingness to fight Claudio for Beatrice.

Elsewhere in the play, love is presented as a battle (in the shape of Beatrice and Benedick) or romantic (in the shape of Claudio and Hero). Love faces obstacles (through the plotting of Don John) but will always win through in the end (the happy ending of the play). Love is presented as important to complete happiness (Benedick's comments to the Prince at the end).

Page 70: Possible Content

- In the extract, Macbeth is presented as brave and honourable for his fighting against the Norwegians.
- He is also respected by the other Lords and the King is grateful.
- However, he is also presented as ambitious and untrustworthy in his aside.

Elsewhere in the play, Macbeth is presented as a man with a conscience (his wish to be a good subject to the King), but easily manipulated by his wife and his ambitions. He becomes paranoid, cruel, and reckless.

Loyalty is presented as something that cannot be relied upon. Despite his apparent loyalty, Macbeth kills his king. Despite being loyal to Macbeth, Banquo ends up dead. The lords' loyalty to Macbeth is tested by his strange behaviour and then his bad leadership.

Page 71: Possible Content

- In the extract, Lord Capulet feels Juliet is too young to be married.
- He wants Paris to wait for two years because he wants the marriage to last.
- He loves her, more so because she is his only living child, and wants her to have a good life.
- He seems a bit of a romantic and wants Juliet to make her own choices in love.
- He tests Paris by inviting him to look at other girls during the party.

Elsewhere in the play, Lord Capulet seems violent (his willingness to fight and his reaction to Tybalt at the party) but is wise enough to try to calm the feud with the Montagues after the Prince's orders. He seems a bad father when he suddenly decides to arrange Juliet's marriage. His attitude towards her when she refuses the marriage is cruel. He is upset after her fake death and, after her real death, wants to stop the family feud completely.

Parents are presented as caring (the Montagues' worries about Romeo) but quite distant and not understanding (we don't see the Montague parents much and Juliet's parents don't listen to her). Parents are often replaced by someone that the child can go to for advice (the Nurse or the Friar). Parents are shown to love their children deep down and regret how their behaviour leads to the death of their children.

19th Century Fiction

pages 72–73

1. For example: *The Strange Case of Dr Jekyll and Mr Hyde* – Utterson, Enfield, Dr Jekyll/Mr Hyde.
2. For example: Pip – nice, lacks confidence, aware of lower social status, close to Joe, loves Estella; becomes a gentlemen, grows ashamed of Joe and increasingly selfish, then regrets his behaviour and makes amends, still loves Estella.
3. For example: Rochester is a member of the 19th century upper class, but doesn't meet their social expectations and is willing to marry 'beneath him'; however, he hides his past sins partly to maintain respectability.

pages 74–75

1. For example: settings in *Great Expectations* – Kent marshes, Pip's house and the forge, Satis House, central London.
2. For example: in *Jane Eyre*, Thornfield shows us a lot about Rochester's character, such as his apparent unfriendliness, his dark secrets, his wealth, etc.

Answers

3. For example: *In The Strange Case of Dr Jekyll and Mr Hyde*, the setting of Dr Jekyll's house represents his facade of social respectability (the front door) and his actual corrupt nature (the side entrance).

pages 76–77

1. For example: *The Strange Case of Dr Jekyll and Mr Hyde* – reputation and respectability, violence, human nature, science.
2. For example: class in *Great Expectations* links to the differences between Pip and Estella, Pip's feelings of insignificance and his wish to be a gentlemen, his changing attitudes towards Joe, etc.
3. For example: the theme of cruelty in *Jane Eyre* links to attitudes towards the poor and towards children in Victorian society.

page 79 Practice Questions

Q1–3.

Level 8–9: a detailed, perceptive and focussed response, presenting a variety of ideas; well-chosen, precise quotations and references; a range of terminology used to analyse the different methods of language, structure and form by which the writer conveys meaning.

Level 4–5: a clear response, mostly focussed on the question, with a number of ideas showing a good understanding of the text; relevant quotations or references; clear explanations of different ways in which the writer conveys meaning through language, structure and form, with some use of terminology.

Q1 Possible Content:

- Physical descriptions of Hyde.
- Descriptions of Hyde's behaviour.
- Hyde's aggressive speech.
- Jekyll's inability to stop changing into Hyde.
- Jekyll's horror at his actions as Hyde.
- The contrast between Jekyll's respectability and Hyde's monstrosity.

Q2 Possible Content:

- Miss Havisham's appearance.
- The setting in which she is placed.
- Her sometimes mysterious dialogue.
- The way she changes when the subject of love appears.
- Her strange behaviour towards Estella.
- When she reveals how she has manipulated Pip and Estella in order to break Pip's heart, and her reaction to his feelings of upset.

Q3 Possible Content:

- How Jane is treated by the Reeds.
- The harsh conditions at Lowood.
- Jane's punishment at Lowood.
- Rochester's treatment of Jane when it seems that he is due to marry Blanche Ingram.
  The treatment of Bertha Mason.

Modern Fiction

pages 80–81

1. For example: *Animal Farm* – Snowball, Napoleon, Boxer, Squealer, Benjamin.
2. For example: Jack in *Lord of the Flies* – aggressive, superior, selfish, instinctive, childish.
3. For example: Jan in *DNA*: loves/needs Phil, wants attention, insecure; as the play develops, we also see a more sensible, caring and moral side to her.

pages 82–83

1. For example: *Lord of the Flies* – power, leadership, human nature, friendship, fear.
2. For example: morality in *An Inspector Calls* – Inspector Goole represents morality, and he challenges the lack of this in the Birling family, managing to make some characters, like Sheila, develop more of a conscience.
3. For example: *Animal Farm* – leadership creates conflict between Snowball and Napoleon; the need to make sacrifices creates conflict between Clover and Molly.

pages 84–85

1. For example: *DNA* – an indeterminate but clearly modern world and the lives of teenagers.
2. For example: *DNA* – the characters can represent any young people in modern society, which is why the characters' names and gender can be changed; each character represents characteristics of, and difficulties faced by, young people.
3. For example: *An Inspector Calls* – the theme of class and justice link to the social position of the working class at the start of the 20th century.

page 87 Practice Questions

Q1–3.

Level 8–9: a detailed, perceptive and focussed response, presenting a variety of ideas; well-chosen, precise quotations and references; a range of terminology used to analyse the different methods of language, structure and form by which the writer conveys meaning.

Level 4–5: a clear response, mostly focussed on the question, with a number of ideas showing a good understanding of the text; relevant quotations or references; clear explanations of different ways in which the writer conveys meaning through language, structure and form, with some use of terminology.

Q1 Possible Content:

- From the start, Cathy doesn't appear to regret what's happened.
- She seems excited by bad behaviour and is excited by the tv coverage.
- She is selfish and greedy.
- Cathy follows whoever is leader and gains their trust so she becomes more powerful as the play progresses.
- She has a very cruel side to her.
- She finally becomes leader.

Q2 Possible Content:

- The initial fight for leadership between Jack and Ralph.
- Jack's treatment of Piggy at different points in the play.
- The conflict that is caused after the fire goes out.
- The confrontation at Castle Rock.
- The final hunting of Ralph.

Q3 Possible Content:

- Gaining power through respect – Old Major, Snowball, Napoleon.
- Power leads to corruption – the pigs' changing of the Commandments; the final scene.
- Power leads to cruelty – Mr Jones, Napoleon.
- Using violence to keep power – the dogs, the trials.

Q4 Possible Content:

- Mysterious.
- Knowledgeable.
- Confident, demanding and confrontational; not intimidated by the Birlings.
- An upholder of justice and morality.
  A mouthpiece for the rights of working class people.

> Expectations of spelling, punctuation and grammar for all exam answers.
> Level 8–9: spelling and punctuation are consistently accurate; a full range of vocabulary and sentence structures are used to effectively control meaning.
> Level 4–5: spelling and punctuation are mostly accurate; a range of vocabulary and sentence structures are used to achieve a general control of meaning.

Index

Acknowledgements

The author and publisher are grateful to the copyright holders for permission to use quoted materials and images.

Images and illustrations are ©Shutterstock.com and © HarperCollins*Publishers*
P.44 © Neil Kirby

P.11, P.12 'Toast' by Nigel Slater (Fourth Estate, 2003). Reprinted by permission of HarperCollins*Publishers* Ltd. © Nigel Slater, 2003.

P.11 Kevin Durant – NBA speech.

P.15 From p8-9 'Autobiography' by Morrissey (Penguin Classics 2013). Copyright © Whores in Retirement 2011.Reproduced by permission of Penguin Books Ltd.

P.20 From *Growing Rich* by Fay Weldon. Reprinted by permission of HarperCollins *Publishers* Ltd © 1992, Fay Weldon.

P.22 © Margaret Atwood 1963, Oryx and Crake, Bloomsbury Publishing Plc.

P.22 *Nineteen Eighty Four* by George Orwell (Copyright © George Orwell, 1949) by permission of Bill Hamilton as the Literary Executor of the Estate of the Late Sonia Brownell Orwell.

P.26 From THE COLLECTOR by John Fowles. Published by Vintage. Reprinted by permission of The Random House Group Limited.

P.48 'Horned Poppy' From THE BOOK OF BLOOD by Vicki Feaver. Published by Jonathan Cape. Reprinted by permission of The Random House Group Limited.

P.53 'Jelly Fish' by Marianne Moore, from *O To Be A Dragon* (Faber and Faber Ltd). Reproduced by permission of Faber and Faber Ltd.

P.53 "Fish" from THE LLAMA WHO HAD NO PAJAMA: 100 FAVORITE POEMS by Mary Ann Hoberman. Text copyright © 1959 and renewed 1987 by Mary Ann Hoberman Reprinted by permission of Houghton Mifflin Harcourt Publishing Company. All rights reserved.

P.54 'You' by Carol Ann Duffy from *Rapture* (Picador 2005). Reprinted by permission of Macmillan.

P.57 'Daughter' by Ellen Bryant Voigt from *The Forces of Plenty* (W.W. Norton & Company, 1983).

P.57 'Her First Week' From THE UNSWEPT ROOM by Sharon Olds. Published by Jonathan Cape. Reprinted by permission of The Random House Group Limited.

P.80, P.87 *Lord of the Flies* by William Golding (Faber and Faber Ltd). Reproduced by permission of Faber and Faber Ltd.

P.80, P.82, P.85, P.87 From *An Inspector Calls* by J B Priestley (Heinemann, 1945) Reproduced by permission of Penguin Books Ltd.

P.87 DNA by Dennis Kelly (Oberon Books, 2009) Reprinted by permission of Oberon Books.

P.84, P.87 *Animal Farm* by George Orwell (Copyright © George Orwell, 1945) by permission of Bill Hamilton as the Literary Executor of the Estate of the Late Sonia Brownell Orwell.

Every effort has been made to trace copyright holders and obtain their permission for the use of copyright material. The author and publisher will gladly receive information enabling them to rectify any error or omission in subsequent editions. All facts are correct at time of going to press.

Published by Letts Educational
An imprint of HarperCollins*Publishers*
1 London Bridge Street
London SE1 9GF

ISBN: 9780008318291

Content first published 2015
This edition published 2019

10 9 8 7 6 5 4 3 2 1

British Library Cataloguing in Publication Data.

A CIP record of this book is available from the British Library.

Publishing Manager: Rebecca Skinner and Emily Linnett
Commissioning Editor: Katie Galloway
Author: Ian Kirby
Project Management: Sarah Dev-Sherman, Q2A Media
Editorial: Jenny Heath
Cover Design: Sarah Duxbury
Inside Concept Design: Paul Oates
Production: Karen Nulty
Text Design and Layout: Q2A Media
Printed by: CPI Group (UK) Ltd, Croydon, CR0 4YY